A REASON FOR LIVING AND HOPING

ADRIAN B. SMITH

A Reason for Living and Hoping

A Christian Appreciation
of the Emerging New Era
of Consciousness

ST PAULS

236

ST PAULS Publishing
187 Battersea Bridge Road, London SW11 3AS, UK

Copyright © Adrian Smith 2002

ISBN 085439 642 X

Printed by Interprint Ltd, Marsa, Malta

ST PAULS is an activity of the priests and brothers
of the Society of St Paul who proclaim the Gospel
through the media of social communication.

Seed Thought

*"The future of humanity lies
in the hands of those
who are strong enough
to provide coming generations
with reasons for living
and hoping."*

Words of the world's Catholic Bishops
at the Second Vatican Council, 1965
(GS.31) echoing Teilhard de Chardin.

Dedication

To the many many Christians I meet who are looking for a vision to live by which their Church is failing to provide.

CONTENTS

Spiritual experience is a common phenomenon
The population-communications factor
The effect of the few
Global consciousness
Our human adulthood
A new cosmology

Jesus, a New Era person
A new way of relating to God
A battle against evil
A universal message

INTRODUCTION

We live in troubled times. No one will deny that. Now, more than ever, we need signs that there is a reason for hope in a better future. Our times are not unique. Throughout history, different peoples in different centuries have experienced periods of desperation, when there seemed to be no hope for a better future. But today the fear is for our future as a human race and this is planet-size. The whole world is crying out for a new vision, an attainable new world order.

It is scarcely recognised that we have, in fact, already been given that vision. It has been preached for centuries but its value to our present world situation is not realised, its appropriateness for our times is not appreciated. I believe that vision was given us by a man from a small village in Palestine who lived in an occupied country and gave hope to an oppressed peasantry. To be empowered by that vision today it is imperative to focus anew on the person and message of Jesus of Nazareth if the Jesus-event is to have any impact on our lives at this time.

We live not only in a different world from that of Jesus — a first century Middle-eastern culture under Greek influence and Roman occupation — but we in the West even live in a culturally different world from our grandparents. Our picture of the Universe and our place in it as one species on a very small planet, and our understanding of our human origins, is entirely different from that of a century ago. How can his vision say anything to us in our fast-developing new paradigm, in our chaotic multi-cultural society with total global communication and the universal fear of terrorism which forms the backdrop of our lives?

To apply the Jesus-vision to today's situation we have to start by mentally extricating ourselves from the everyday world in which we are enmeshed in order to obtain, as it were, a satellite picture of what is going on, of what are the influences playing on our lives, of how we might interpret the crises of our times as the birth pangs of a new era. This is what we will consider in Part One.

In Part Two we will have a close look at the vision Jesus proclaimed in terms of the Kingdom or Reign of God[1]. His 'programme' has been lived in two stages and is now entering a third. The first stage was very short, during the three or so years when Jesus manifested his vision. He saw his life's work as making known to his fellow Jews — by his own way of life as much as by his message —that God was calling them to live by higher values than those the contemporary Jewish religion was offering. He believed the way forward was to have a direct relationship with God without the need of mediators, priests and go-betweens. In fact, that the time of formal religion was at an end (Letter to the Ephesians 3: 12). Certainly he had no intention of launching a new religion upon the world. He believed that the new 'Reign of God' was immanent and that his coming would see the fulfilment of God's plan for creation: the end time. He

---

1. The phrase *Kingdom of God* is not one that attracts people today to explore the vision to which Jesus awoke us. Some authors have used *Kindom* or even *Queendom*! But I shall continue to employ *Kingdom* because this is the word used in translations of Scripture. We will look at the expression's meaning in more depth in Chapter 5.

had, therefore, no need of disciples to carry on his work into the future: no need for what we call the Church. He opposed the hierarchical, patriarchal structures of society.

His views were so in advance of his time that they are still hardly recognised even among Christians today. His was a message of how we were called to live in a loving relationship with God, and with each other. However, the expected end did not come. His followers tried to live out his ideals, one group within Judaism (the Jerusalem community under St James' leadership) while the other group, under St Paul's leadership, took the message out to the non-Jewish world. With the sacking of Jerusalem by the Romans in the year 70CE the Jerusalem community withered and the form of Church we have today blossomed out of the mission of St Paul and his disciples.

The proclamation of the Reign of God became interpreted in terms of Greek philosophy and became a 'theology'. The message *of* Jesus became a message *about* Jesus. The Jewish prophet became idolised and named first the Son of God and later God the Son, a title that would have been repugnant to his Jewish beliefs[2]. During

---

2. Although 'Son of God' was perhaps the most important New Testament title for Jesus, we have to understand it as having much less theological weight in Hebrew culture than it is given in the Church. Among the Hebrews the title was given to an individual or group who was perceived to be close to God, under God's protection. The Jewish nation as a whole was called God's Son (Psalm 2:7), as was a devout believer. In a special way the title belonged to the King of Israel (2 Samuel 7:14). When the title is applied to Jesus in the New Testament Letter to the Hebrews (1:5 and 5:4-5) — 'You are my Son; today I have become your Father' — it is in this same sense, as a specially chosen person, the author quoting Psalm 2:7. So to speak of Jesus as 'Son of God' was to speak of his significance rather than of his origins. Jesus himself uses the expression this general way in the Beatitudes: 'Blessed are the peacemakers: they shall be called sons of God" (Matthew 5:9).

Only after the Council of Nicaea in the 4th century did the phrase take on the Trinitarian meaning we give it today in the Creed as 'only begotten Son of God'. In fact, at Nicaea the phrase 'Son of God' was promoted to mean 'God the Son'.

this second stage, over the last two thousand years, his message has become privatised. We have been concerned with a Jesus who was sent to be the saviour of our souls. His Good News was understood as being about preparing for the next life and has largely been confined to the Church.

The present decline of the influence in the West of the once powerful Church marks the end of the two-thousand year Christian era. The main-line Churches are now described, with their dwindling influence on society and falling membership, as side-line Churches.

Today we are entering a third stage of understanding the Good News. Or rather, we are returning to understand its social dimension, its power to build a better world, its concern for justice, its community dimension. To release its power for our own day we have to re-think the Jesus-event in terms of our contemporary western culture. That means in the light of what quantum physics is telling us about the inter-connectedness of all things, of all humanity, in the framework of our place in a vast Universe, in the setting of globalisation, in the relationships between world religions, and with an emerging secular spirituality.

In Part Three we confront the characteristics of our world today (Part One) with the vision Jesus shared with us of his understanding of God's design for humanity (Part Two) and discern how each of us might further that design in our everyday lives.

PART ONE

Interpreting Our Times

"At the root of the major troubles in which nations are today involved, I believe that I can distinguish the signs of a change of age in mankind."

— Teilhard de Chardin
The *Moment of Choice* (in *Activation of Energy*)
Christmas 1939

1

WHAT'S NEW?

'Death', people say, 'is the only certainty.' Surely not. Change is the only certainty of which death is one mode of change. Change is of the essence of all life, moving through cycles of birth, growth, maturity or blossoming and then eventually death, after which human beings move on to a re-birth in another dimension of life. But, as the majority of the world's population believes, only after a series of re-incarnations on Planet Earth. Who knows? Nobody knows because nobody has ever come back from any imagined celestial abode to tell us of what lies ahead after we have passed beyond the barrier of death. But that is not our concern now. Our living in a more human way here on Planet Earth is our concern.

Change on Planet Earth is not a closed circle. While it is cyclic, it is evolving. A symbol might be a spiral staircase, going round and round but rising at the same time. Where change is evolving, the new will emerge. Most obviously, humanity has recently changed from a pre-technological society to a technological one, from a pre-scientific age into our present scientific age. It is arguable, as we will see below, whether such change is from a less to a more perfect state of being, whether it can be named 'development', if human happiness and fulfilment are the criteria.

17

Change can be seen also in the manner in which human beings organise their relations with other human beings on the cultural and political planes. Because part of the essential nature of the human being is to be drawn towards forming relationships, there has been throughout history the tendency to relate in larger and larger groupings. From nomadic families to settled tribal units in villages to larger and larger villages, from towns into cities and in the last centuries into conurbations. Only two hundred years ago less than 3% of the world's population lived in cities of 20,000 or more. Today more than half of humanity is living an urban existence. Tribes have come together to form distinct peoples (we speak of the twelve tribes of Israel considering themselves as 'The People of God') then to form nations and nation-states which have made alliances together, or the stronger have conquered the weaker, to form Empires, until today we have continental-wide groupings: the European Union, the Organisation of African Unity right up to the United Nations with its one hundred and ninety-three member countries.

There is continuing change too in the way in which human beings relate to the natural environment, to the world of the supernatural and, more recently, to our understanding of our own consciousness. We will look at these in turn.

RELATING TO OUR ENVIRONMENT

Environmentalists are talking about 'sustainability'. It is the first time we in the West have had to face the fact that we can no longer live in the way to which we have become accustomed. We will be forced to change our lifestyle, to relate to nature in a new way.

The word that has come into common usage to describe our way of relating to the rest of nature is 'ecology'. It comes from the Greek *oikos* meaning 'household'. We consider ourselves to be the householders of our planet. In the early seventies the Norwegian philosopher, Arne Naess, made a distinction between what he called 'shallow' ecology and 'deep' ecology. This is a tremendously important distinction because the shift from the former to the latter epitomises the breakthrough humanity is currently making from our traditional — and present — paradigm to a totally new way of understanding our world and humanity's place within it. A 'paradigm' has been defined as the fundamental way of perceiving, thinking, valuing and doing associated with a particular vision of reality. It is our vision of reality which is undergoing a monumental change in our present time, causing us to perceive and understand ourselves in our relationships — to other people, to our planet and to the Transcendent — in an entirely new way.

Our world view for the last centuries owes a great deal to the writing of Sir Isaac Newton (1642-1727). His theory was a breakthrough at the time but his clockwork simile of the world, with its presumption that at the foundation of everything were basic building blocks (the unsplitable atom) upon which everything was built and that the whole edifice operated to discernible and unchanging laws, just does not match with the way physicists understand Planet Earth today.

Quantum theory in physics — developed since the nineteen twenties — is largely responsible for this shift of paradigm. We have split the atom and gained entry to the sub-atomic level of existence, to the world of leptons, electrons, muons, neutrinos, not to mention neutrons and protons! causing us to realise that we can no longer deal with 'things' but only with things in relationship. Quantum Theory gives us a new appreciation of creation, a holistic understanding. There are not inorganic bits of matter but a web of energies: all is interconnected and interdependent. Sub-atomic particles act not according to laws but only according to probabilities. All being is both wave-like and particle-like but just which it is at any given moment is unpredictable.

To return to Arne Naess' distinction, what he calls 'shallow' ecology is a product of the traditional, Newtonian world view in which everything was understood as human-centred. In this perspective humanity is above and outside the rest of nature because we consider ourselves as the pinnacle of creation, the most superb of all creatures. We are in control. We perceive everything else as having a value only in relation to us and their value is a *use* value: how useful or not this or that is for us.

This attitude gave rise to and in turn was enforced by the religious traditions of the West, Hebrew, Christian and Moslem. We humans, in this view, are God's ultimate and supreme creation 'made in the image of God'. On that basis we flatter ourselves by thinking of God as the Being that has all our human qualities to an infinite degree. We really make God to our image.

The concept of humanity's evolution being marked 'progress' is challenged by Paul Davies in his book *The Fifth Miracle*. He says it implies a value judgement, for instance that humans are better than apes. We use adjectives like 'higher' mammals or 'lower' vertebrates. He writes:

> Just what is it about humans… that makes them an improvement on other organisms? In terms of sheer numbers, microbes

20

win hands down. If adaptational success is the key criterion, superbugs are pretty adept at coping with environmental stress. Humans, of course, have high intelligence. That makes us successful when it comes to IQ, but we are hopeless swimmers and we cannot fly. If we decide that intelligence is what matters, we are undeniably at the top of the ladder. But is this not simply a case of chauvinism? We ourselves have selected the criterion that makes us top.

Yet what poor specimens we are! One of our specialities is killing each other. There are many instances of one-to-one combat in the animal world but in most cases such fights among members of the same species do not end in death. As soon as one animal realises it is losing it retreats and the other allows it to go. This is something we have obviously forgotten on the path of evolution from animal to human being!

Such shallow ecology, picturing humanity's dominance of the Earth — a very male, macho image — created the hierarchical social paradigm which has predominated human society for some 4,000 or even 5,000 years. The hierarchical paradigm has power issuing from the top and trickling downwards. It accounts for patriarchy, for racism, for imperialism, for exploitation and for religious superiority: all those attitudes which cause some people to regard themselves as superior to other people. The very word 'environment' means our surroundings: it presumes we are at the centre, more important than these surroundings.

And yet hierarchy as a pattern of social relationships is entirely a human mental construct. It does not exist in the rest of nature. It is we who project it onto nature.

We shall be looking at this again in Chapter 8 in the context of the shape society should take if it is to live by the values of God's reign which Jesus announced.

Deep ecology, on the contrary, understands humanity as being part of the total natural environment. All living beings, and the non-living too, have the same intrinsic value. All are willed by the Creator: all have a part to play. Everything in nature is fundamentally interconnected and interdependent.

Shallow ecology can be called a materialist's view of nature, valuing it by what is useful, while deep ecology can be said to be a spiritual vision. We find this vision among the Aborigines, the North American Indians, the Celts, among all pre-technological people who do not make the distinction we in the West make between the sacred and the profane. They had a deep reverence for Spirit dwelling in and energising everything. They were able to recognise that everything, but everything, contained a spark of the Divine.

All the major problems of our time, whether in the field of politics or economics or religious division, cannot be understood — and certainly not remedied — except we understand them in the wider picture as interconnected, not only with each other but with what has gone before and with our vision for what we hope will come.

RELATING TO THE SUPERNATURAL

The traditional ecological paradigm, with all power at the top of the pyramid, placed God at its summit, in fact above its tip. Our very word 'super-natural' says it all. There is that which is above and beyond the natural, and consequently outside nature, outside creation.

The three monotheistic religions of the West, Judaism, Christianity and Islam, are characterised by a supernatural theism. Their God is completely transcendent.

Within Christianity this reached its ultimate expression in the 18th and early 19th century with the theology of Deism: that God is entirely non-immanent, like a clock-maker who manufactures the clock in the first place, winds it up for perpetuity, and then lets it run on according to its nature.

In the Middle Ages Theology was regarded as the 'Queen of Sciences'. Dealing with matters beyond creation it could provide the ultimate answers to all our questions because understanding came to us through Revelation from the Divine Source.

We find quite the opposite understanding of the Divine in the great eastern religions. Their key word is 'immanence', expressed in western theological terms as Pantheism, whereby all that exists is God and God is all that exists.

Today, western theologians are finding a middle way. Yes, God is transcendent, the Creator is apart from what is created, but yes too, God operates, energises creation from within it, is immanent as well. To name this, theologians have coined the word 'panentheism': the *en* meaning *in*. With this scenario we might say that Cosmology, understood as the story of the origin, the evolution and the destiny of the Universe which enables us to make sense of our lives, is the present day 'Queen of Sciences'. It is Cosmology that is integrating physics, biology and astrophysics.

RELATING TO OUR OWN CONSCIOUSNESS

Along with the human sciences of anthropology and sociology that have developed over the last century is, of course, psychology. As Descartes used the clock as a metaphor for the body and its workings, today we use the computer as a metaphor for the brain. I shall be writing more about the recent expansion of human consciousness in the next chapter, but at this point I want to state where I stand in the current controversy on mind-brain relationship. Some authors equate the brain with the mind, with consciousness. I quote as one such Francis Crick who with James Watson discovered the structure of DNA in the fifties for which they received the Nobel Prize in 1962. He writes: 'The Astonishing Hypothesis is that "You", your joys and your sorrows, your memories and your ambitions, your sense of personal identity and free will, are in fact no more than the behaviour of a vast assembly of nerve cells and their associated molecules' *(The Astonishing Hypothesis: the Scientific Search for the Soul)*. 'Is it reasonable,' a reviewer of that book asks, 'to say that the best way to study a Rembrandt is to start by examining the molecules of paint on the canvas?'

I affirm that while the brain is physical, a part of the body, the mind, our consciousness transcends the physical. One has only to read the growing collection of reports of 'out of the body' experiences. How else explain how a physically blind person on a hospital operating table can 'see' and later report on what was going on during the operation and even describe the colours in the room when in an 'out of the body' experience at that time? The mind is not a 'thing' but a process, whereas the brain is a structure. A brain is not necessary for a mind to exist. A plant has a mind, a consciousness, which orders its growth, shape, colour, etc, according to its DNA, but it has no brain. At death our brains wither but our mind, we believe, continues into a spiritual realm. From this we can postulate that our consciousness is non-local, it is not bounded by time or space.

The shift we are making at the present moment can also be understood in an ecological perspective as an emergence from an industrial growth society, characterised by its accelerating consumption of the Earth's natural resources, to a life-sustaining society. How rapidly this ecological revolution will take place — whether, indeed, it will come about in time to save Planet Earth from an approaching destruction — depends upon a change in consciousness on our part, of we who populate the planet today. Are there signs of this? Glimpses of a new attitude to economics can be seen in the wind farms of Denmark, the solar rooftops of Japan, the paper recycling mills of Germany, the steel recycling mills of the United States, the irrigation systems of Israel, the reforested mountains of South Korea and the bicycle networks of the Netherlands.

At present our world is ruled by economics. Economics emphasises competition, expansion, domination: all attributes of a hierarchical, patriarchal society and indeed of the astrological Age of Pisces. Whereas Ecology emphasises co-operation, conservation, partnership, all traits of the Age of Aquarius, which astrologers tell us we are entering at present.

Changes in any form, whether of attitudes or customs, take a long time to be universally accepted. The diagram on the next page illustrates the process. It is reckoned that the really inspired, creative people form only 2% of a population but they are by temperament the least likely to convert their dreams into reality. However, their vision is quickly picked up by the intuitive people who sense that the vision is right: a further 10%. This 12% represents the critical mass which is able to launch the idea widely. It is quickly picked up by another 30%

25

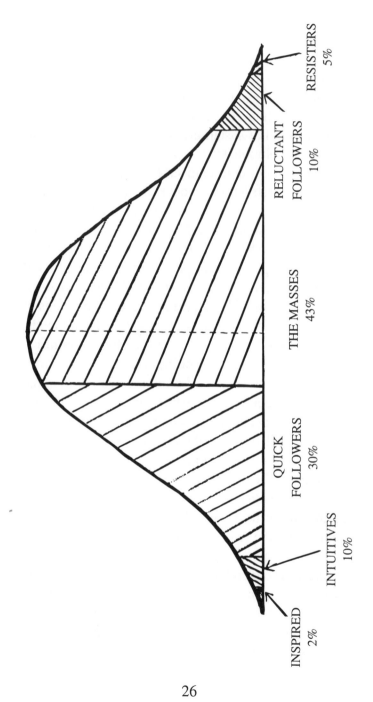

RESISTERS
5%

RELUCTANT
FOLLOWERS
10%

THE MASSES
43%

QUICK
FOLLOWERS
30%

INTUITIVES
10%

INSPIRED
2%

which number has the ability to broadcast the vision so that soon it is embraced by the next 43% and so becomes that of the majority. By then "the new thing" becomes part of local or national life. There will always be those who are suspicious, those reluctant to change, the 10% who will eventually be sucked into "the new thing". But always too there is the small percentage who are vehemently opposed: the resisters.

It is interesting to compare this pattern with what research in the USA is finding in regard to our present ecological revolution.

> 75% say: 'we are going to need major changes to live sustainably.'
>
> 60% say: 'we want to change'.
>
> 25% are 'downshifters'. They are already making a change by disengaging from the rat race of the consumer society.
>
> 10% (in the USA that is 20 million people) have gone further and are pioneering a new way of life that is more sustainable and satisfying.

It is said that in Britain 25% of the population are making positive changes.

Such a change of attitude to lifestyle is the only way to save our planet from its present woes: climate disruption, destruction of the protective ozone layer, deforestation, poison by pollution.

If attitudes are to change, if a new consciousness is to evolve, it will not be through fear of the consequences of the dangers listed above. It can only come about through a positive vision. We Christians have such a vision, a blueprint of what life on Earth could be like if all human possibilities and potentials were allowed to develop. Jesus presented us with such a blueprint. He called it 'the Reign of God'. In other words, the world as God designed it to be.

Before familiarising ourselves with this design of God we need to examine the changes that are presently happening at all levels of society. To take stock, so to speak, of where we are in the western world at this present time. As a first step, let us take a bird's eye view of the social and cultural changes that have taken place among us within our own life-time, to see if we can identify an emerging new paradigm.

RECENT SOCIAL AND CULTURAL CHANGES

It is now widely held that the *1960s* were a turning point, giving us the first signs of something new breaking through. It was the decade of the Hippies and Flower Power. We began to hear the term *New Age* which was, and still is, an umbrella label for a whole range of events, programmes, activities, fashions and philosophies that did not fall conveniently into any previous classification. We heard of the Beetles going to sit at the feet of Maharishi Mahesh Yogi, the teacher of Transcendental Meditation, and of our Aunt Susan surreptitiously attending Yoga classes (purely to lose weight, of course). The Body, Mind and Spirit Exhibitions began to draw larger and larger crowds of people looking for something 'alternative'. But at the same time these 'New Age' phenomena — and many were not new at all but a return to an appreciation of some centuries-old activities of native peoples — were regarded as very 'fringe' to society in general. However, it was about more than a new lifestyle. It produced a new appreciation of matters spiritual and religious.

On the Church scene, the World Council of Churches was publishing its reports on new attitudes to evangelism *(The Church for Others)* which presented a new image of the Church as being in and for the world instead of a refuge from the world. At the same time the world assembly of Catholic bishops, sitting as the *Second Vatican Council*, was thinking along the same lines. This new thinking not only gave impetus to the nascent ecumenical movement but opened up dialogue with other world religions.

But perhaps the feature of this decade which made the greatest impact on the human psyche was the first photograph of Planet Earth taken by the USA Vanguard II space probe on 17 February 1959. Gone was our image of the world as we had always seen it on our classroom globes with their political boundaries and empire colouring. We were seeing the most beautiful, delicate object hovering in space, with its oceans and forests and deserts in blues and greens and browns. We looked at it with wonder as the home, the only home, of the whole human race.

During the *1970s* this vision of Planet Earth caused a shift in our ecological consciousness from a utilitarian attitude towards lifeless material resources to perceiving the whole planet as a living organism, to understanding that the entire cosmos is a unified system. It was in this decade that James Lovelock, a marine biologist who had worked with NASA on their space programme, published his theory *(Gaia: A New Look at Life on Earth)* that Planet Earth functions as a single organism which maintains conditions necessary for its survival. He named it *Gaia* after the Greek mythological goddess 'Mother Earth' who bore Uranus.

New social trends were beginning to emerge. People were beginning to lose confidence in all forms of hierarchical institutions and there was a general questioning of authority, among the student population especially. With an increasing decline in traditional religious involvement there arose a growing interest in discovering a personal meaning and purpose in life and a search for an existential spirituality. There emerged a greater tolerance of ethnic, sexual and political differences and the role of women was becoming more prominent because of a rise in appreciation of the feminine values.

Far from being passing fads, these features, looked upon as fringe to society in the 1960s were becoming a recognisable part of our culture by the *1980s*. This was the decade that saw the publication of seminal books analysing our times such as Alvin Toffler's *The Third Wave*, John Naisbitt's *Megatrends*, Fritjof Capra's *The Turning Point* and Marilyn Ferguson's *The Aquarian Conspiracy* which put names to the personal and social transformations that were taking place in the West. Ecological and environmental awareness was spreading with more people taking seriously the consequences of global warming, the depletion of fossil fuels, the rapid disappearance of so many animal and plant species. And not unrelated to this we notice the rise in the number of young people becoming vegetarians (5% of the population of Britain today) for a variety of reasons, not least because they found the eating of once-living flesh abhorrent. Self-improvement courses seemed to mushroom. Brochures promoting self-awareness holidays on Greek islands arrived through the letter box and the corner shops had more cards in their windows advertising a whole range of alternative therapies.

While schools of meditation (of the eastern kind) were springing up in our cities the Church saw the appearance of the books by Matthew Fox *(Original Blessing* and *The Cosmic Christ,* for instance) which expressed what a lot of Christians were intuiting, that a new and positive Cosmology, Universe story, was needed if we were to make Christian revelation relevant to our present moment of history. It took the name *Creation Spirituality.*

During this last decade, the *1990s,* we were not surprised to notice whole sections of the larger bookshops labelled 'New Age' or 'Body, Mind and Spirit' and to see an unprecedented birth of glossy magazines devoted to New Age subjects. We noticed that what were previously referred to as Alternative Therapies had become Complimentary Medicine. Chinese medicine shops were opening in most towns and lectures on every conceivable 'personal development' subject were on offer all over the country — often at considerable expense! While a variety of psychological studies of our evolving consciousness started appearing in the form of novels (such as *The Celestine Prophecy* and *Mutant Message Down Under)* academic journals were launched *(The Journal of Consciousness Studies,* for example) publishing erudite papers on a subject that had by now become the concern of a number of university faculties. As Duane Elgin wrote *(Collective Consciousness and Cultural Healing)*: 'Now as we enter the communications era, humanity is making another quantum leap in collective consciousness as our observing or knowing capacity is being turned back upon itself. We are becoming conscious of consciousness as a species'. And Dom Bede Griffiths wrote: 'There is a whole movement in physics today recognising that matter cannot be separated from consciousness. We are at the beginning of an extremely important moment in human history' *(Transcending Dualism.* A public lecture given in Jerusalem, 1983).

CURRENT PHENOMENA

To bring us up to date perhaps I can do no better than simply to list a sample of the numerous characteristics of today's shift in consciousness:

— The valuing of partnership, collaboration and pluralism.
— The aspiration of young people for authenticity.
— The information explosion and increasing reliance on computers.
— The experience of pluralistic, multi-ethnic societies.
— Uniformity giving way to an appreciation of unity in diversity.
— The collapse of long-standing political and ideological barriers.
— A greater freedom from customs, taboos and ethical parameters.
— A growing interest in esoteric disciplines and Shamanism.
— A movement from curing (an ailment) to healing (the total person).
— The self-assurance to challenge long-held beliefs and codes of behaviour.
— An increasing value being given to larger communities (UN, EU, OAU, etc.)
— An urge to re-connect with the body: emotions, feelings, imagination, intuition.
— Increased concern for justice, human rights and the suffering of others world-wide.
— The demand to participate in decision-making: a decrease in the willingness to be controlled by the powerful few whether in politics, industry or the Church.
— A re-awakening to the value of Celtic spirituality.
— A steady rise in the tourist industry and access to travel by more and more people.
— The emergence of new forms of community-living and communes.
— More research into and wider possibilities of genetic engineering.
— An increasing awareness that Nature has a value of itself and not just in terms of its use to human beings.

—The growing desire for networking, ranging from the Internet to the exchange of ideas between groups.

—The application to increasingly more areas of life of the theories of quantum physics.

—The wider influence on our minds by the media.

—An increasing global financial inter-dependence.

And this is no more than a sample list.

In one of his encyclical letters Pope John Paul II recognised these trends in society:

> As the Third Millennium of the Redemption draws near, God is preparing a great springtime for Christianity, and we can already see its first signs. In fact both in the non-Christian world and in the traditionally Christian world, people are gradually drawing closer to Gospel ideals and values, a development which the Church seeks to encourage. Today in fact there is a new consensus among peoples about these values: the rejection of violence and war; respect for the human person and human rights; the desire for freedom, justice and brotherhood; the surmounting of different forms of racism and nationalism; the affirmation of the dignity and role of women. *(Redemptoris Missio* N. 86. 1990).

THE NEGATIVE SIDE

But we would be looking at our world through rose-tinted glasses if we did not recognise all the negativity that is also around us.

First, there is the immense suffering caused by so many natural disasters — earthquakes, floods, droughts — which appear to be on the increase in proportion and frequency. Our response to these might be to shrug our shoulders and simply say: 'That is nature. There is no way we can control that'.

One can lay the blame for much on global warming — and given enough good-will, we can do something about that — but I believe there is another more subtle connection relating human behaviour to natural disasters. As is becoming increasingly clear to scientists, every aspect of creation is interconnected, interdependent, every action has a cosmic effect. The enormity of evil caused by humanity — and we human beings are the sole cause of evil: animals can do no wrong, they can only behave according to their nature — must surely be having its repercussions on the natural order, the cosmic forces.

Secondly, on a world scale we witness the number of man-caused (and I mean 'man') conflicts, inter-tribal wars, the genocide we politely call ethnic cleansing. Since the establishment of the United Nations in 1945, for 'nation to speak peace unto nation' there have been over a hundred and fifty major wars. And the present situation looks more threatening than ever. Then there is the suffering imposed on the Third World by the greed of the First World. Every minute one million dollars is spent on arms. If there was a moratorium for two weeks enough money would be released to pay for all the food and health needs of the entire world population for a whole year. And so on and on.

All this may alarm us, but should it surprise us? We are in a time of transition. Historians point out that at the time of any major cultural evolution, as has occurred in the great civilisations of the last five thousand years — Egyptian, Syrian, Hellenic, Roman — the social symptoms are always the same. Namely, a sense of alienation, an increase in mental illness, violent crime, social disruption and an increased interest in religious cultism.

But why do we seem to be in an apparent deadlock to escape from this negativity? How do we get out of this cycle of violence? In his book *Losing Control: Global Security in the Twenty-first Century,* Paul Rogers coins

34

the word 'liddism' (to keep the lid on in order to prevent the pot boiling over) to describe what is happening. He makes the point that political and military orthodoxy in the developed world still insists that the principal threats to its security are such things as ethnic and religious fundamentalism, organised crime, terrorism, drugs, Third World corruption and misgovernance, the spread of small arms, the emergence of chemical and biological weapons. And the orthodox solution lies in maintaining national defences and military alliances, erecting even higher fences to keep out undesirable immigrants and moves to prevent the developing world getting hold of the kind of weapons that 'we' already possess.

These are but symptoms of a much deeper malaise: the gulf between the pursuit of national interests, which the elected politicians of the West are expected to uphold, and the global interests which transnational corporations, environmentalists and the World Bank and IMF have as their goal. So say the economists.

I propose that this gulf will never be bridged if these concerns remain at the level of intellect. The human intellect is helpless to solve problems of its own making. Our politicians and world leaders are trying to solve a right-brain problem with a left-brain approach. These problems can never be solved at the level of the mind, but only at the level of spirit. As Einstein said, you do not solve a problem by means of the things which caused the problem. We can only rise out of the present impasse by our dealing with it out of a higher state of consciousness. Walter Wink writes in *The Powers that Be:*

> Only by confronting the spirituality of an institution and its physical manifestations can the total structure be transformed. Any attempt to transform a social system without addressing both its spirituality and its outer forms is doomed to failure.

Materialism knows nothing of an inner dimension, and so is blind to its effects.

▽ There is no need for nations to do battle over the world's goods. They abound in plenty. What we are lacking is the good will to share them.

It is this desperately needed change of perspective that is the subject of the chapters which follow.

2

A New Consciousness

'It is no secret today to the careful observer. Humanity stands at a turning point. We could even say that we find ourselves in the midst of a transformation of such dimensions that it occurs only once in millennia.' So wrote the German Jesuit and Zen Master, Hugo Enomiya-Lassalle in the 1980s.

The energy that underlies the accelerating changes within our lifetime that we reviewed in the last chapter has been caused by the evolving among us of a new and deeper consciousness.

> Humanity today finds itself in a crisis at the crossroads between the old consciousness and the new. Today, standing at the threshold of a great evolutionary shift, we encounter the dawn of a better world. A profound transformation is occurring in our thought, our value systems and in our perception of ourselves and our environment. Indeed we speak nowadays of a "paradigm shift".

This was written by Roland Ropers in 1986, introducing the book *Living in the New Consciousness,* by Hugo Enomiya-Lassalle.

Before we proceed we need to recognise that there is a difficulty with the word 'consciousness' because it can have so many meanings for which in English we have only the one word. To be 'conscious' can mean simply being awake, alert in a medical sense, or it can mean being aware of a fact or phenomena at a deeper level than perceiving. We can use the expression 'self-conscious' to mean embarrassed or to mean being self-reflective about one's own existence: the very ability which differentiates the human mind from the animal mind. Consciousness is something we are so immersed in that we live unaware of it. To ask what it is is like a fish asking what water is. It is found in every living form down to amoeba level. It is fundamental to the Universe. All our knowing about everything is taking place in our consciousness.

In the ancient Indian language of Sanskrit there are some twenty different words for consciousness, each with a different level of meaning. Here I shall use the word to mean *that activity of the mind in which all human experience takes place.* It is our very ability to have experience.

As with every evolutionary step, the new consciousness does not just begin with a bang but develops from the small seeds which are the ideas of that 2% of creative thinkers. Names of such thinkers which come to mind are Pierre Teilhard de Chardin, C.G.Jung, Abraham Maslow, Carl Rogers and Aldous Huxley.

OUR PARADIGM SHIFT

A paradigm shift such as this is not simply the next step in a process of invention or education, like moving up to a higher form in school. It is not just an adding on to the old, but the taking of a step in a new direction. This is to take a risk because it means letting go of the former paradigm. Thomas Kuhn, the creator of the phrase 'paradigm shift' says: 'The transfer of allegiance from paradigm to paradigm is a conversion experience that cannot be forced'. One cannot operate from two paradigms at the same time. Two people of the past who took the risk of a leap into a new paradigm were Copernicus in the 16th century and after him Galileo. To shift from a paradigm in which the Earth was the centre of the Universe to that of a Sun-centred or Solar System — and accept all the consequences — was a shift indeed and they were rewarded with the mockery and wrath of those who could not accept the shift. The writings of Copernicus were placed on the Papal Index of forbidden books and Galileo was hauled before the Inquisition and forced to 'abjure, curse and detest' his absurd views. These shifts are not born of more knowledge but of a new way of thinking. They burst forth from a sudden intuition.

One notices a number of recurring themes in the writings over the last couple of decades about the emerging new consciousness, which we can list as characteristics of this phenomenon:

1. That there will be a great bursting forth of our potential, physical, intellectual and spiritual: a development of human resources we hardly knew we had.

2. That the Universe is shot through with living intelligence. That Planet Earth is one living system, Gaia, which has a self-regulating ability to provide the constant and optimum conditions for the survival and development of life on Earth. That humanity is part of this single system.

3. That being part of it, we have to live in harmony with, rather than to use, and abuse, creation. We are not the owners of but partners with nature. Hence the increasing ecological awareness.

4.   That the consciousness of human beings is tapping into the global consciousness of our planet, bringing about a spiritual awakening and a raising of our level of awareness to cosmic consciousness.

It is with this last that we are particularly concerned here.

Many authors attribute the new consciousness to an increase in intuitive (as different from rational) thinking. And this in turn they attribute to a shift from predominantly left-brain thinking to an increase in right-brain thinking.

The brain has a left and a right hemisphere. The left hemisphere analyses, discriminates, measures, names and organises. Its thinking is lineal going from A to B to C, from cause to effect. The right hemisphere sees in wholes, synthesises, unites, detects patterns, comprehends the totality of A to Z. It is the creative, imaginative, non-rational part of the mind. The former is said to predominate in the masculine mind and the latter in the feminine.

Our western culture has, since the sixteenth and seventeenth centuries favoured rational knowledge over intuitive wisdom, science over religion, competition over co-operation, always enforced by our patriarchal society. Today, we notice, there is a move to redress the imbalance, not by letting the pendulum swing the other way but by cultivation of the whole brain. This is coming about by more people taking up the different practices of deep meditation and also by a deliberate education policy to cultivate the creative, unifying, non-competitive potential of children. Teachers and parents so often remark to me that today's small children seem to be much more 'aware', 'connected', 'together', 'centred' than they themselves were at that age.

Among adults too there are signs of a rapid increase of the number of people with a holistic view of life. A fascinating study of social change in the United Kingdom over the last few years divides the population into three main groups. These are Sustenance Driven people who are motivated by the need for security and cling to an existing lifestyle, Outer Directed people who are motivated by a search for esteem and status, and the Inner Directed who are motivated by self-actualisation, preferring quality of life to quantity of possessions. K. MacNulty (*UK Social Change through a wide-angle lens*) illustrates these three types by the reasons they would give for eating less:

The Sustenance Driven:	'Because food is so expensive.'
The Outer Directed:	'Because I want to look good in my bikini'.
The Inner Directed:	'Because I feel better for it.'

The third group was hardly noticeable forty years ago. Today they form one third of the population of Britain and Denmark, 40% of the Dutch, 26% of Germans and are foreseen to be increasing rapidly while the other two groups are diminishing. A recent survey in the USA, where the three categories are named Traditionalists, Modernists and Culturally Creative respectively, reveals that 23% of the population consider themselves to be in the third category.

The inner-directed is the group which is most concerned with social and ecological issues, causes health-food shops to boom, is suspicious of genetic engineering, believes that change comes about in society through a growing individual awareness and has a tendency to hold spiritual values while shunning organised, conventional religion.

41

In his book *Putting on the Mind of Christ* Jim Marion compares the seven levels of consciousness of the human personality — ranging from the 'Archaic Consciousness' of infants to the 'Subtle Consciousness' of the fully enlightened person — to the stages through which the human race evolves. Following the 'Magical Consciousness' of children, is the third stage 'Mythic Consciousness' of pre-adolescence followed by 'Rational Consciousness' of the teenager. He makes the point that Mythic Consciousness has been the dominant and average consciousness of Christian believers. Their beliefs are expressed in mythic terms, for example, in the Creeds. Characteristic of this level of consciousness is the belief that provided they keep the rules, respect the roles and accept the mythology, they will be saved. 'So Christianity, despite what Jesus and his disciples said and wrote, was soon reduced to the level of mythic consciousness and, for the most part, has stayed that way, at least at the popular level, for most of these last two thousand years.'

Rational consciousness, Marion maintains, is the dominant consciousness of our present western society. Out of this level comes the theological thinking of most of the clergy who rationalise Christian myths and the Good News, and theologise about the person of Jesus. The raising of human consciousness from the mythic to the rational level has been the spiritual task of Christianty's great saints and theologians: the early Church Fathers, Augustine, Thomas Aquinas, Ignatius Loyola, Francis de Sales, to mention just a few. Marion believes that in our time increasingly more people are moving into a higher state of consciousness. He calls this level 'Vision-Logic Consciousness'. He describes its characteristics as those of right-brain thinking. There is a change of energy so profound at this time that every level of reality is shifting its energetic resonance.

Of particular interest to us is that this shift is regarded as extremely threatening by the predominantly rational-consciousness Church leaders and especially by the Christian fundamentalists whose awareness remains at the mythic level. Both groups are showing increasing signs of panic that 'the world is going to the devil'. (How this move from mythic or rational consciousness to the emerging level of consciousness affects the loyal Christian as an individual, we will consider in Chapter 12.)

Many Christian writers are recognising the emergence of this new consciousness as a dynamic force. (See the next page.) Just as there is no way to stop our exploration of outer space now that it has been set in motion, so there is no way now of holding back our exploration of inner space. This was foreseen by the Jesuit paleontologist Pierre Teilhard de Chardin in the 1940s. While the word 'biosphere' is used to denote the inter-relationship of all living beings on our planet, Teilhard used the word 'noosphere' (from the Greek word noos, 'mind') to refer to the interconnection of all human minds right around the globe and the cumulative effect of their interconnectedness. (It was actually Professor Wladimir Wernadski, living at the beginning of the 20th century in Moscow, who created the notion of Noosphere.) Teilhard pictured the Earth as enwrapped in a human, reflective, planetary layer of consciousness daily becoming more and more complete, leading to what he called 'planetisation' and sometimes 'hominisation of the planet'.

If this seems far-fetched, let us look at the growth of the collective memory and information bank of the human race. While the faculty of memory develops within each human being it is also contributing towards and able to tap into a collective human memory. The traditions of

Some Christan Authors Who Recognize That We Are Moving into a New Era of Consciousness

Teilhard de Chardin
A great many internal and external portents (political and social upheaval, moral and religious unease) have caused us all to feel, more or less confusedly, that something tremendous is at present taking place in the world.

The Future of Man. p. 82. 1942

As the most authoritative scientists admit (Haldane, Julian Huxley, and so on) the Universe, as now revealed to us by facts, is moving towards higher states of consciousness and spirituality.

Introduction to the Christian Life (in Christianity and Evolution. p. 151). 1944

Hugo Enomiya-Lassalle
(It) is certainly no secret today to the careful observer. Humanity stands at a turning point. We could even say that we find ourselves in the midst of a transformation of such dimensions that it occurs only once in millennia.

Living in the New Consciousness. p. 3 1988

Denis Edwards
At the end of the Twentieth Century, we are moving into a new phase of evolutionary history.   *Creation, Humanity, Community: Building a new Theology. p. 5. 1992*

Thomas Merton
We are living in the greatest revolution in history, a huge, spontaneous upheaval of the entire human race.

Conjectures of a Guilty Bystander. 1968

Bishop Stephen Verney
There can be little doubt that we stand on the edge of a new epoch.

Into the New Age. p. 8. 1975

F.C. Happold
Something is happening in our world. We are conscious of it all around us. We are now on the verge of one of those mental and spiritual leaps which have happened before in the history of mankind, eras when the corporate mentality and spirituality of man shift and expand and new vistas and interpretations of the Universe open up.

Religious Faith and Twentieth-Century Man 1966

Bede Griffiths
The world today is on the verge of a new age and a new culture... There is a general feeling today that we are at the end of an age...

A New Vision of Reality. 1989

I feel that we are on the eve of a new breakthrough in consciousness, of a new wave of civilisation.   *Letter to HW. Dec. 22, 1972*

44

our past and of each culture are stored and transmitted in language, educational systems, libraries, museums, codes of law, religious traditions, rituals, schools of philosophy and theories of science. For previous generations such stores of information have been in this or that geographical place, often in a specialist library. Today, by means of the Internet this great human memory bank is becoming available to any individual in any location.

Already sixty years ago Teilhard named two phenomena as contributing to the growing global consciousness. The first was the *phenomenon of unemployment.* He showed how life has always developed 'by releasing psychic forces through the medium of the mechanisms it has devised' and points to 'the growing number of people able to use their brains because they are freed from the need to labour with their hands'. He goes on: 'The attempt to suppress unemployment by incorporating the unemployed in the machine would be against the purpose of Nature and a biological absurdity. The Noosphere can function only by releasing more and more spiritual energy with an ever higher potential'. He named as a second characteristic of the present age which is contributing to the development of a universal consciousness, the *phenomenon of research.* 'Research, which until yesterday was a luxury pursuit, is in process of becoming a major, indeed the principal, function of humanity'. Today, tens of millions of people are employed in some form of research.

Teilhard maintained that evolution proceeds by what he called the law of Complexity-Consciousness. By this he meant that as the basic energy of the Universe organises itself into ever more complex patterns, it manifests an increasingly higher level of consciousness. So humans, being more complex than other vertebrae, have a higher level of consciousness.

He saw the relational development of the human mind as a further step in the evolution of the human species, towards a new level of human society, a super-society, which would experience a global consciousness. He referred to the fulfilment of this process, the end point towards which we are converging, as the 'Omega Point'.

A contemporary of Teilhard's, a Cambridge-educated Indian mystic, Sri Aurobindo, invented the term 'Supermind' for what he believed was the next stage of evolution from matter to life to consciousness. It is to be so far beyond our present consciousness that it is the ultimate evolution of 'Spirit', but it will come about through the increasing spiritual growth of individual consciousness.

CONSCIOUSNESS STUDIES

Scientists too are recognising that after three centuries of mechanistic science, consciousness is a legitimate area of scientific enquiry. Several universities have recently established a faculty of consciousness studies. We know how the brain works but consciousness still remains a mystery. The view that consciousness is a cause of phenomena and not an effect has been advanced by, among others, the neuro-psychologist Sir John Eccles, the quantum physicist David Bohm and the biologist Rupert Sheldrake.

What indications are there that this New Era of Consciousness is coming to fruition now in our own time? I believe there are two indications: one mathematical and the other astrological.

Peter Russell, in *The Awakening Earth* develops the interesting comparison, made four decades earlier by Julian Huxley (published in the *Scientific Monthly* in

1940) between the growth of the cells in a human brain and the quantitative growth of human brains in the world as 'cells' of a global brain, a brain of brains. The human brain in the womb develops in two stages. Eight weeks after conception the number of nerve cells in the brain increases by many millions each day. After five weeks this process slows down. Then follows the stage during which billions of isolated nerve cells begin to make connections with each other. By the time of birth a nerve cell may communicate directly with several thousand or even as many as a quarter of a million other cells.

The average human brain contains some 100 billion nerve cells (neurons) of which ten billion are in the cortex, the area associated with conscious thought processes. Brains with only one billion or fewer neurons, such as the brain of a dog, do not have the ability that humans have of self-reflective consciousness. Only a brain the size of a human cortex allows the exercise of this faculty.

Our Planet is now populated by six billion brains. The increase of population has been occuring in ever shorter intervals of time. It took from the appearance of the first human being,

> until 1830 to reach 1 billion,
> until 1930 to reach 2 billion (100 years),
> until 1960 to reach 3 billion (30 years),
> until 1975 to reach 4 billion (15 years),
> until 1986 to reach 5 billion (11 years)
> but until 1999 to reach 6 billion (13 years).

The United Nations estimates that the world population will stabilise at 10 billion in the year 2080, and the fact that it has taken thirteen years to reach the last billion would seem to indicate that the pace of growth is slowing down. Twenty years ago the average size of the family world-wide was 4.7 children. Today it is 3.

Ten billion seems to be the critical figure for a new level of evolution to emerge. There are this number of atoms in a single living cell and this number of cells in the cortex of the human brain. However, Russell believes that we will not have to wait a further eighty years because five billion is already well within the necessary range. So the first stage is complete!

The second stage depends on building up the intercommunication between the nerve cells, or, on the global scale, between the human brains. With the fantastic speed of increase in communications it is foreseen that with the present rate of data processing — the information on the Internet doubles every six months — the global telecommunications network could soon equal the complexity of the human brain. It should be noted, however, that this calculation is based only on the external means of communication. In the next chapter we will be saying something about the Morphic Resonance built up by increasingly more people developing higher states of consciousness and the effects this has on other people and on the environment.

ASTROLOGICAL AGES

The other indication that the New Era of Consciousness is coming to fruition in our time comes from the science of Astrology. This accounts for the fact that the emerging era is often referred to as the 'Age of Aquarius'. Reference in this context to the Signs of the Zodiac is not so esoteric as it might seem.

The cardinal signs of the Zodiac, namely Taurus, Leo, Scorpio (often portrayed as an eagle) and Aquarius, were adopted as the symbols of the four Evangelists. Four English cathedrals — Chichester, Carlisle, Lincoln and

Canterbury — incorporate zodiac symbols in their architecture, as do at least nineteen pre-Reformation parish churches from Kent to the Isle of Man. How else would we have St Matthew's story of the 'Wise Men' who came from the East to visit the new-born king, unless their wisdom had been in astrology?

Which of us has not, at least from time to time, looked at the daily paper to see what advice or warning our 'sign' is offering us for that day!? Besides, if we believe that the whole Universe is shot through with living intelligence, it is logical to accept that the forces that maintain the galaxies affect life on this planet, and to endeavour to interpret these influences.

Everyone knows that the gravitational pull of the Moon influences our tides and of the effect a full moon can have on some minds — animal as well as human. It is less well known that scientific tests have revealed that trials of extra-sensory perception (ESP), for example telepathy, succeed much better when Planet Earth is on one side of, and closer to the edge of, our galaxy — so the time when there is very little of the galaxy directly overhead — while when there is a great deal of the galaxy overhead, they do badly. We are more influenced than we realise, or care to admit, by our relationship to other stars and planets.

In these first years of the new millennium astrologers tell us we are moving into a period when we will be influenced by the energies issuing from the triple conjunction of the planets Uranus, Neptune and Jupiter. In astrological terms Uranus is related to breakthroughs and revolutionary changes of a life-enhancing nature. (Uranus was prominent at the time of the breakthroughs made by Newton, Descartes, Freud, Jung and Darwin.) Neptune is related to the dissolution of boundaries and with mystical awareness, while Jupiter tends to expand and magnify everything with which it comes into a relationship.

Astrologers divide the Earth's complete orbit of the Sun — one year of 365 days — into twelve segments each with its own Zodiacal sign. They usually take the Spring (Vernal) equinox, March 21st, to be the beginning of the astrological year. So we have in turn the Vernal Equinox (Aries, Taurus, Gemini), the Summer Solstice (Cancer, Leo, Virgo), the Autumnal Equinox (Libra, Scorpio, Sagittarius) and the Winter Solstice (Capricorn, Aquarius, Pisces). What is less well known is that the whole of our solar system, of which our Planet Earth is a part, moves through the heavens in a gigantic orbit of 26,000 years. This vast period of time is known in India as 'A day in the life of Brahman' (God). Astrologers divide this great cycle too into twelve sections, each of approximately 2,100 years during which our planet moves through the signs of the Zodiac but in the opposite direction. Jewish astrologers of pre-Jesus times, according to the Rabbinical writer Abarbanel, believed that the Messiah would appear in Israel when there was a conjunction of the planets Saturn and Jupiter in the constellation of Pisces. Today, astronomers in their planetaria can turn the stellar clock back to reproduce the sky as it was on any day, month or year. They have discovered that there was such a conjunction in December of the year 7 BCE. This provides us with a marker for the begining of the Age of Pisces.

In a fascinating booklet, *God and the New Age*, the Rev. Dr. Kenneth Cuming shows how many indications there are in the Bible to this and previous ages. For two thousand years before Abraham, the Age of Taurus (sign: the winged bull) this animal was the object of worship in

50

Egyptian religious culture in the Minoan and Cretan civilisations and in Assyria. When Abraham was inspired to leave Ur of the Chaldees, about 2,000 BCE, he was moving not only from one land to another but from the worship of the winged bull to initiate the next great age, that of Aries the Ram. The story goes that it was a ram that he sacrificed in place of his son, while the Paschal Lamb had a great significance for his descendents from the Exodus onwards. The animal was not any more the object of worship but the symbol of sacrifice. Are we perhaps to understand the erecting of the Golden Calf in the wilderness not only as an act of idolatry but as an attempt to thwart God's design for his Chosen People by turning the clock back to a previous age? Right up to the time of Jesus the ritual slaughter of rams and lambs continued to be a central act of daily Temple worship.

The birth of Jesus the Christ ushered in the next great age, that of Pisces, the Fish. We cannot help but notice how prominent the fish was in New Testament times. Apart from ninteen passages in the Gospels referring to fish and the promise of Jesus that the apostles were to become 'fishers of men', the fish became the great Christian symbol of the early Church, appearing first in Alexandria around the year 200. The letters of the Greek word for fish, *ichthus*, were ingeniously seen to be the initial letters of the Greek words for *Jesus Christ, Son of God, Saviour.*

And now we are another 2,000 years on, entering the Age of Aquarius whose symbol is a person pouring out a pitcher of water. Is this the age marked by the outpouring of the Spirit of creativity? We are reminded of the words of the prophet Joel:

> 'I shall pour out my spirit on everyone:
> Your sons and daughters will proclaim my message;

51

your old men will dream dreams,
and your young men will see visions.
At that time I will pour out my spirit on servants, both men
and women' (2:28-29).

In his book *Putting on the Mind of Christ* Jim Marion makes some interesting observations about the way in which human consciousness has evolved — particularly in humanity's relationship to the Divine — during these four astrological periods. The stages of humanity's evolution are epitomised in the stages of an individual's human growth today.

The Taurus Age, 4,000-2,000 BCE, was a time when people lived in tribes. Their many gods and goddesses, who seemed to act quite arbitrarily, were largely nature gods who had to be offered sacrifices, including human sacrifices, to be appeased. The basic attitude towards these deities was one of awe and fear. People were not valued as individuals but as making up the tribe. This stage of evolution is mirrored in the consciousness of today's child aged between two and seven who does not yet think of herself as having individual personality. The small child appeases her parents to get her own way. Marion points out that this level of consciousness is also reflected in how some Christians regard Redemption. Jesus is understood to be the victim sacrificed to appease God on behalf of humanity: such a sacrifice is so supreme, because of who Jesus was, that there is nothing more required of us.

During the Aries Age, 2,000-0 BCE, tribes came together and empires were formed. Polytheism gradually gave way to monotheism and the one god was a male sky-god. There was an increasing value being given to the individual and the sacrifice of humans was abandoned in favour of animals. (That was the lesson being given in the story of Abraham, stopped at the last minute from sacrificing his son.) God was not so arbitrary, but a God of laws: who, in Hebrew history, made a contract, a covenant, with his people. Moses gave the Israelites commandments and laws to regulate their life together as a people. This period is equivalent to the child from seven to adolescence. She is beginning to understand herself as an individual but is in need of rules and regulations to give her security, to be able to know right and wrong. Some Christians reflect this level of consciousness in their understanding the Redemption as the sacrifice of the Lamb of God which was required to fulfil the law of justice.

The last two thousand years — the Age of Pisces from which we are now emerging — is equivalent to the years following adolescence, an age of abstract thinking. Our God is a loving father rather than a judging God. When Jesus chased out of the Temple the money-lenders and stall-holders selling animals for sacrifice with the words: 'The Scripture says "It is kindness that I want, not animal sacrifices"' (Matthew 12:7) it was a symbolic act marking the end of the Age of Aries, inaugurating the age of 'love thy neighbour as thyself'. During these centuries this love has been expressed particularly by external deeds. The Cross is understood by Christians of this level of consciousness as a symbol of sacrificial love.

And now, in the third millennium, we are entering the Age of Aquarius, the Age of the Spirit, a period of inner evolution of human consciousness. A time of human maturity, a period in which humanity's relationship to God will be expressed less through the outward observance of religious ritual, which *The Way* of Jesus has become, but more in an inner encounter through a deeper consciousness. Astrologers characterise the Age of Aquarius as one of harmony, high moral idealism and spiritual growth. The Cross is coming to be seen as symbolic of that interior death and resurrection each of us has to make to break through to the fulness of the Kingdom of God.

I close this chapter with a quotation from *Towards a Global Ethic: An Initial Declaration* of the Parliament of World Religions meeting in Chicago in 1993:

> Earth cannot be changed for the better unless the consciousness of individuals is changed first...[And] without risk and a readiness to sacrifice there can be no fundamental change in our situation.

We will see in Part Three how this Age is challenging the Church to change.

WHY NOW?

3

Why, one reasonably asks, should such a fundamental, evolutionary change be taking place at this particular era of human history? Why now and not in the time of our parents or even our grandparents?

Each of the previous major evolutionary leaps — from self-replicating molecules to simple cells (the first forms of life) to multicellular organisms, to plant life, to aquatic life, to emergence from the sea, to animal life on land, to the formation of our earliest human ancestors — each of these developments came about, in the physical order. The evolutionary shift of our own time, precisely because it is a shift in consciousness, pertains to another order. It can only come about consciously. That is, when willed by us. It is precisely the development of our consciousness which is what is new. The leap we took out of the mythical Eden from sub-consciousness to self-consciousness is now being followed by a further leap to super-consciousness. We are evolving from a physical to a metaphysical vision of reality. As I wrote in a previous book *(The God Shift)*: 'We are moving beyond the limitations of our rational minds, beyond what we learn through our five senses, beyond the frontiers of space and time, to the exploration of inner, deeper realms. We are stretching the boundaries of our consciousness. It is at this point in our history that we are moving beyond our physical potential to explore our spiritual potential.'

So to answer the question 'why now?' we have to look for reasons which relate to our expanding consciousness. There is no one single reason, one dynamic force which is bringing this about. But there are a number of momentous changes that are happening simultaneously and because of the web of all life, progress in one field accelerates progress in all fields. In other words, the shift is caused by a number of factors all influencing one another at the same time. Let us have a look at some of these.

THE MILLENNIUM FACTOR

The effect of a change in our calendars can too easily be dismissed as a cause of any evolutionary effect on life. After all, what has been celebrated? Simply a conventional way of calculating time, and in particular that method of calculating time known as the Gregorian Calendar. It is only one of many. The Jews number their days from the first day of the creation of the world as calculated from the books of Moses, so the Christian year 2000 was 5760-5761 for Jews. The Islamic year consists of twelve exact lunar months and the Islamic calendar is dated from the flight of Mohammed from Mecca to Medina. The Hindus, the Chinese, the Japanese have their own calendars and there are others as well. Ours is not even a universal calendar for Christians. Coptic Christians, for example, retain the Alexandrian calendar which dated the years from the beginning of the rule of Diocletian in 284 CE. It was a Scythian monk, Dionysius

Exiguus (Denis the Short) living in Rome in the 6th century who first suggested that our years should be dated from the birth of Jesus, to replace the Alexandrian Calendar. Why should the western calendar, the Gregorian Calendar, be so important? In itself it is not. It is not even an accurate calculation of the birth of Jesus upon which it is supposed to be based. But it is the most influential. It is used world-wide for transport, for communications, for financial transactions. So wherein lies its power to change life so fundamentally? After all, dates and months have no meaning in the natural world. The answer lies in the word 'synergy' from the Greek *syn-ergos* meaning 'to work together'. It is the energy created by combined action, whether physical or mental action.

The human brain, as we saw, contains billions of neurons, or nerve cells, and with each thought that comes to the mind, the neurons produce a miniscule amount of energy. Where hundreds or thousands of people — hundreds or thousands of minds — are gathered together, all wishing or thinking the same thing in coherence, an energy is produced that can actually bring about a psychological or even a physical effect. Which of us has not been caught up in a mass of like-minded people, whether at a football match or in a protest rally, and found ourselves 'contaminated' by the crowd around so that we are drawn in to share the same enthusiasm or outrage? An example often quoted to illustrate this effect are the Nuremberg rallies of Hitler in the 1930s when the mass energy generated completely conquered the minds of individuals.

There is a tendency deeply embedded in the human psyche to expect that the future will always be better. It is observable in history that when our ancestors have been faced with a new century there has been an expectation that new and better things will come about. Humanity seems always to be looking forward to a Golden Age. The human being has an innate longing for an age of peace and love, of justice and plenty. Millenarianism has constantly reappeared in one form or another: the belief in a future period of ideal happiness. Our New Testament book of Revelation (chapter 21) holds out the promise of a new Jerusalem: the vision of 'a new heaven and a new earth' and in II Peter we read: 'We await for what God has promised: new heavens and a new earth, where righteousness will be at home' (3:13). It seems that we are incapable of living fully in the present because we regard the present as a low point between the high of a Paradise at our origins and the high of the Kingdom of Heaven in the future.

The turn of a century, or in our case of a millennium, is not therefore the cause but the occasion of a world-wide expectancy of the new, the better. Such expectancy created by billions of minds in synergy the world over creates a physical energy that can actually be creative of what is expected.

THE SEARCH BEYOND THE MATERIAL

Another factor we have already touched upon in the previous chapter, is the growing number of people who are moving beyond the desire to possess more, to have more material goods, towards giving priority to the spiritual aspect of their lives. A poll taken in 1995 revealed that 80% of Britains believe our society has become too materialistic. An element of this shift is an increasing move away from regarding science as having the last word in explaining all we know, to a realisation that there is much more, the intangible, the non-measurable, beyond science.

This new concern for the spiritual is not the same as an interest in or return to formal religion. It is important to make this distinction between the two. Over the last decade I have been working with a great many groups on areas of spirituality. I have always asked them what they mean by the word 'spirituality' because it is widely used these days to cover so many different experiences. Unlike religion, which is a human creation, spirituality is innate to the human person, disposing us towards finding a meaning in life. It transcends religion. Putting together the main ideas that come up in these groups, I have arrived at the following which can be no more than a working definition because spirituality is concerned with mystery.

Spirituality is that dimension of our nature — related to the physical and psychological dimensions — which awakens us to wonder, gives our lives meaning and calls us towards our higher self, usually expressed as a relationship with the Transcendent (sometimes named 'God').

Religion, on the other hand, which has been a feature of human life only recently — for little over three thousand years of the two million years of human existence — is a particular framework which includes four characteristics (a belief system, a moral code, an authority structure and a form of worship) within which people find direction and nourishment for the spiritual dimension of their lives, and explore their spiritual journey in the company of others.

We cannot be non-spiritual because that is part of our condition as self-reflective creatures living on a time-space Earth. Our condition invites us — compels us — to relate: to relate to other human beings, to relate to all else on Planet Earth and to relate to the beyond time and space. The very word *religion* comes from the Latin root *re-ligare*, to bind together.

The externals of religion evolved slowly in human history as did other cultural features:

1,600,000 BCE	Homo Erectus;
600,000	Discovery of fire;
400,000	Homo Sapiens;
150,000	Dwelling in caves;
100,000	Ability to use language, use of stone blades, emergence of modern humanity with self-reflective consciousness;
60,000	*Evidence of religious ritual, especially in burial customs;*
30,000	Development of art;
20,000	Flute music. *Signs of explicit religion*;
15,000	First houses;
10,000	Horticulture. *Female-only deities;*
5,000	Script writing. Towns began to grow into cities of 10,000 inhabitants;
4,000	Agriculture. *Male gods predominate*;
3,600	*Temples.*

It would appear that only from about 20,000 BCE onwards — in the last 1% of humanity's existence on Earth — are there any signs of explicit religion, the emergence of cults with a system of gods, priests, worship, sacrifice and divine and priestly kingship. Only in this period does there appear to be any speculation about the gods and their powers for good and evil in the Universe.

In other words, it is only comparatively recently in our human history that the major religions, as we know them today, began to appear, Hinduism being the first, around 2,000 BCE. Formal religion comprises only about 6% of the history of the human religious story. Judaism emerged only around 1,200 BCE. The centuries 600-300 BCE saw a decisive step forward in human consciousness in both East and West. Karl Jaspers (1883-1969) the German existentialist, in his book *The Origin and Goal of History*, calls it the Axial Period because human culture seemed to make a great shift on its axis. It produced the great sages: Gautama Buddha, Lao Tzu, Parmenides, Zoroaster, Pythagoras, Socrates, Plato, Aristotle, Patanjali, Confucius, the sages of the Upanishads and the Hebrew Prophets. It was the period of the birth of the other great religions: Zoroastrianism, Taoism, Confucianism and Buddhism. (Islam, of course, followed much later, 600 CE, from the roots of Judaism.) And it was the period that saw the building of the Parthenon in Athens, the Temple of Solomon, the Lighthouse of Alexandria and other great monuments. It was the period which saw the birth of philosophy, thanks to the Greeks and the Athenians in particular, and of mathematics, music, all the arts, especially the theatre and what we would today call science. It was the dawn of democracy and citizenship.

The late appearance of formal religions in human history causes us to ask how necessary they are to human life. Are they a phenomenon of a transient stage of human evolution out of which, perhaps, we are now passing in our progression to a higher state of consciousness? The very idea of religions as separate communities is a comparatively modern invention. In none of the great religious scriptures, nor indeed in any other than Western languages, is there a word which corresponds to our Western concept of 'religion'. The word is found in

Western languages because, with our dualistic way of thinking, we contrast 'religion' with 'secular', 'spiritual' with 'material', 'holy' with 'profane'. In other parts of the world there is a unity of life and the religious dimension does not exist apart from all the other aspects of life.

Is St Paul's famous chapter on Love (I Corinthians 13) telling us that ultimately what counts is each person's spiritual experience? Creeds and doctrines are a religion's attempt to explain the cause of and to interpret the meaning of that spiritual experience which is common, in varying degrees, to the whole of humankind. In Europe, since the Middle Ages the search for meaning has moved from Church control to Mind control to Scientific control. (See diagram opposite) In our own time the pendulum is swinging back to the spiritual element of human life, but not to institutionalised religion.

Irrespective of formalised religion the human person has the capacity to transcend towards a richer, fuller sense of wholeness. God is present in the act of perpetual creation and God's Spirit is present within every human being, causing each person to be a spiritual being but not necessarily religious.

SPIRITUAL EXPERIENCE IS A COMMON PHENOMENON

It was Alister Hardy, a biologist, who proposed the hypothesis that experience of God is 'a biological fact'. In 1984 the Alister Hardy Research Centre was set up at Manchester College, Oxford, to collect, monitor and analyse accounts of religious and spiritual experiences in individuals, regardless of their religious context or affiliation, to test Hardy's hypothesis. He had previously set up a Religious Experience Research Unit in 1969 and

MIDDLE AGES

CHURCH CONTROL

Bible	— Tradition —	Theology (Queen of sciences) ("Science" = Nature & Body)
		Albert the Great
		Thomas Aquinas

The RENAISSANCE & the ENLIGHTENMENT

MIND CONTROL

Galileo	Newton	Descartes	Francis Bacon
Sun-centred	*Clockwork Universe*	*Rationalism*	
		Dualism	*Secular science*

18th & 20th CENTURIES

SCIENCE CONTROL

Secularism	*Industrial age*	*Scientific age*	*Evolution*
Materialism		Einstein	*Quantum physics*
		Darwin	*Astro-physics*
			Human sciences
			Genetic engineering
			Information Highway
			Global village

63

this unit had studied more than 4,000 case histories of individuals who had had some form of religious experience. A similar research carried out at Nottingham University on a national scale with 2,000 people suggested that more than 30% of the adult population of Britain has had such an experience. The experiences recorded, drawn from people in all walks of life, include being bathed, surrounded or suffused in light, which is variously described as pure, white or brilliant, accompanying strong flashes of insight into the nature of self and the Universe, or feelings of inexplicable release and joy. 'It does not appear true, as Freud would have had us believe, that religious experience is associated with mental imbalance or weakness', said Edward Robinson, the Centre's Director at the time. 'It is much more associated with psychological maturity and personal integration. Nor is it associated, as Marx said, with the downtrodden and the oppressed, but on the whole with people who are well-adjusted, and even comfortable in their lives.' The existing evidence is sufficiently varied for Robinson to suggest that essentially religious experience is the same, no matter from what tradition it comes.

A later Director, David Hay, said that when they did more detailed in-depth studies, but still on random samples of smaller groups (eg. university students, adult citizens of Nottingham, nurses in Leeds) the positive response rate went up to over 60%, but about 40% had not told anyone else about it, not even people as close as husband or wife. They were frightened of being labelled mentally unbalanced.

In 1975 the National Opinion Research Corporation in the USA reported that more than 40% of American adults polled believed that they had had a genuine mystical experience.

So, religious or mystical experience is no more connected with a religion than is salvation — and it is certainly no monopoly of Christianity. It can be experienced by people with no previous spiritual awareness, that is, awareness of the realm of the spiritual, as differentiated from the physical or mental. The experience does, however, lead to an awareness of the spiritual dimension. (J.M.Cohen and J.F.Phipps have collected together a vast number of such experiences in their book *The Common Experience*.) The danger lies in people interpreting such experience, as was the case in the Middle Ages, as a recognition by God of the person's sanctity, or, equally dangerous, in the opposite way, in attributing mystical experience to some evil force or to its personification, Satan. Sanctity is measured by a person's love of humanity. One can be whole without being holy and holy without being whole. Some of the greatest saints were quite neurotic!

It is a characteristic of our present culture that while more people are searching for a spiritual meaning to their lives, they are not looking for it in a religious context. With some friends I launched a decade ago the 'More-to-Life' retreats, and against the advice of people in the communications business we advertised them as 'non-religious guided retreats'. 'You should never advertise with a negative', they warned. In fact it is precisely the negative that has continued to attract people to them. They write to tell us they want space to explore their spiritual journey but that they do not want anything 'churchy' or doctrinal.

Dom Bede Griffiths, the Benedictine monk, writing from his ashram in Southern India, said: 'We are moving out of a materialist civilisation centred on science and technology into a new age in which people all over the world are consciously turning to a spiritual path'.

While lecturing on this subject I often put up this quotation on the screen: 'The spirit inhabits the whole cosmos, gives breath to all life and tunes our hearts to hear the heartbeat of the earth and the way of truth and beauty', and I ask the audience to guess the source. From a Church document? From the Scriptures of another Faith? From a well-known spiritual writer? They are surprised to be told that the source is not religious but secular: the United Nations Conference on Environment and Development in Rio in 1992.

THE POPULATION-COMMUNICATIONS FACTOR

The third great influence on our times is the fact that the world population has now reached six billion.

Recall what we said in the last chapter. For the very first time there are on Planet Earth a sufficient number of brain-boxes (six billion) to take us beyond the critical figure required to create a 'global brain', a Noosphere, as Teilhard de Chardin named it. The second stage of the process, corresponding to the growth of the human brain, is the need to build up a network between the brain cells. At the physical level this is happening through the development of the different forms of telecommunications. This is often referred to as the information explosion, or even the information over-load. Every person in every part of the globe now has the possibility of retrieving information upon anything from any source. This is knowledge-availability networking.

But at the same time there is the increasing amount of networking happening at a deeper mind level: more people living with a deeper awareness, or 'mindfulness' as the Buddhists call it, often by practising some form of deep meditation: Yoga, Zen, Sufism, the hypnotic chanting of mantras or a variety of techniques offered by the different schools of meditation. What they all have in common is to provide a means for the mind to rise to a higher state of consciousness.

Higher than what? In normal everyday living human beings operate in one of three states of consciousness. They are the state of deep sleep when the body and the self-reflective mind are totally at rest, so deeply in fact that we are unaware that we are in this state at the time and only realise that we have been in it when we wake from it. This is not to say that our consciousness is not active. It continues to regulate our body functions causing us, for instance, to turn over from side to side. Secondly there is the twilight state, the dream state, when the body is at rest and the mind relaxed and not under conscious control, but nevertheless we are aware of all sorts of imaginings or disconnected thoughts passing through the mind. The third is the wakeful, alert state in which we spend most of the daylight hours, when both body and mind are active and influencing each other.

Beyond these, most authors describe four further states which go by various names and are less clearly defined. For instance, Transcendental Consciousness (or pure awareness), Cosmic Consciousness (which is a permanent state of the former), God Consciousness (which is not a consciousness *of* God but rather 'seeing' creation in its totality, its 'inside' and its 'outside') and Unity Consciousness. The point I am making is that increasingly more people are employing one or other technique to transcend the three lower, everyday, states and so enter higher states. These higher states effect a synergy, a coherence among the minds in these states and so bring about a networking of brain-boxes at a very deep and powerful level.

But why am I suggesting that the phenomenon of increasingly more people taking up a meditation practice should be contributing to our evolution to a new state of consciousness? Because the new era into which we are entering is not primarily a time of new social concern, nor of increased global politics nor of more just economies — though each of these may be an eventual outcome of our new paradigm — but it is precisely a raising of consciousness.

The exaggerated use of our left-brain, rational approach to life's problems which has dominated the Western world's thought processes for so many centuries, is now being balanced by the cultivation of more right-brain intuitive thinking. And the practice of deep meditation is one of the main contributory factors because it is a holistic, balancing exercise.

THE EFFECT OF THE FEW

But, we might ask, is this practice becoming so widespread as to have a world-wide influence? I can speak only of one such technique from personal experience and shall draw my examples from that: Transcendental Meditation (commonly referred to as TM) as taught by Maharishi Mahesh Yogi. The movement currently claims that some three and a half million people have been taught this technique world-wide since the 1950s when Maharishi first introduced it to the West under the title of The Spiritual Regeneration Movement.

To what extent are the effects of TM measureable? The physical effects on the individual meditating — the changes in the EEG (electroencephalogram) patterns indicating the relaxation of the nervous system, the slower rate of heart-beat, a drop in the rate and volume of breathing and the fall in the metabolic rate (the rate at which the body burns up its fuel) — can all be measured scientifically by repeated control tests.

The effect upon the environment, however, can be measured only circumstantially rather than scientifically and therefore with less certainty. Such environmental effects as the lowering of stress and its consequences can be observed in areas where 1% of the population is practising TM. Such are, for instance, a decrease in the crime rate, a drop in the number of hospital admissions, a fall in the number of accidents, less violence. There is no way of knowing, however, whether these measurable effects are due simply to the percentage of people of a given area practising TM, as the TM organisation would claim, or whether they are also the consequence of a number of people practising regular deep meditation in a variety of ways, including, for instance, the presence in the area of a monastery of contemplative monks or nuns. But whatever the form the practice takes, how do we explain the connection between the exercise of this small minority and the observable facts?

The theory that explains this connection goes by a variety of names: Morphic Resonance, The Morphogenic Field, Formative Causation, and in the case of the TM movement, the Maharishi Effect. The theory is that when only a small percentage of people make a breakthrough in consciousness this empowers vastly more people to make the same breakthrough.

Do we not notice that children today learn to ride a bicycle almost spontaneously whereas we of the older generation acquired the art only after many a spill? Even allowing that cycles today are of an improved design, can we not say that the facility seems to be so widely transmitted that it has become an automatic part of our human mechanism? Are we not today witnessing a generation picking up a facility with computers which will be passed innately to coming generations?

People practising deep meditation often find that their meditation experience is more profound when meditating in a group than when they meditate alone. Furthermore, experiments have revealed that when a large group of people were meditating together — in this case Transcendental Meditation — a smaller group a thousand miles away experienced an increased coherence between the individuals while they meditated, even though they did not know at what time the larger group was meditating. That is to say, the pattern of brain activity of the second group was more in tune with each other than usual. It is as if during meditation people are setting up resonating electromagnetic waves around the planet.

Dr. Rupert Sheldrake, a biochemist, has built up a theory, which he calls Formative Causation, of how life evolves, from experiments in the plant and animal kingdoms in which he has observed the same effects. For instance, when a collection of rats has learned a new pattern of behaviour, other rats, all over the world, tend to learn the same behaviour more easily.

In the Autumn of 1984 he conducted an experiment on the 'Tomorrow's World' programme of BBC television. A member of the audience was asked to choose between two pictures made up of blotches. To most people in the audience the image in the chosen picture was impossible to identify (*see opposite page*). This picture was then shown to viewers and the image revealed. So there were now two pictures: one largely incomprehensible and the other revealed to an estimated eight million viewers. During the following weeks the two blob pictures were shown to six thousand people in Britain and in twelve other European countries who had not seen the television programme. In continental Europe 33% of people who were shown the picture that had been revealed to viewers in Britain were able to recognise what the blobs showed, while there was no significant change in the small percentage able to recognise the meaning of the undisclosed blob picture.

The fact of transmission over a distance of thoughts, consciousness, energy, even evil intent, is not new to us. We call it telepathy. In the Middle Ages in Europe and still in Africa today, evil can be wished upon an absent person by sticking pins in a doll. The results are remarkable!

GLOBAL CONSCIOUSNESS

Today we are understanding these influences in terms of global consciousness. What we notice is that numbers seem to play a critical part. Maharishi claims that if 1%

This is the hidden-image picture that was shown.

71

of the world's population were practising TM the course of history would be profoundly altered. (Through many years of scientific research the Maharishi International University in Iowa, USA, has found that the formula required to create coherence in the collective consciousness of a given population is for the square-root of 1% of that population to be practising the powerful TM-Sidhi programme.) George Gurdjieff, the Russian mystic and teacher said that just 100 fully enlightened people would be sufficient to change the world.

Even in the Hebrew Scriptures (Genesis 18:23-32) we find an illustration of the spiritual influence of the few upon the many, albeit told in terms of an interventionist God. Abraham pleads with the Lord to spare the city of Sodom from destruction if only a handful of just men can be found among the guilty inhabitants. After a lot of bargaining by Abraham, the Lord promises to spare the city if there are found as few as ten just men.

During 1986 a group based in Texas calling itself the Planetary Commission for Global Healing attempted to reach 'the critical mass of human consciousness' by enlisting five hundred million people in seventy-seven countries to spend an hour in 'healing meditation' at twelve noon local time on December 31st so that there would be a twenty-four hour period of meditation being done by 10% of the world's population. They claim that the number reached eight hundred million in 1987. During 1988 we saw peace 'break-out' in more places than we have seen in recent decades. A coincidence?

Whatever doubts we might have about the validity of statistics for particular occasions we must surely agree with the views of the late Sir George Trevelyan:

> Though he is but a tiny unit in himself, man meditating is performing a deed of cosmic significance. By each medita-

tion we align with the universal process. Man is the catalyst that can allow the redemptive events to occur, so that the Spirit can impregnate the body of Earth.

OUR HUMAN ADULTHOOD

A fourth factor of contemporary life contributing to our planetary shift in consciousness is that we are now more fully in control of our lives, of our environment, than ever before. I state this simply as fact, not wishing to make any value judgement upon it. Whether we are more fully human thereby or not, is another question!

Does greater control necessarily equate with greater maturity? I believe our maturity must be measured by the manner in which we exercise our power to control. That humanity today — in the Western world at least — does exercise greater control is particularly evident in two areas of our lives: in technology and in politics.

During the years I spent living among villagers in the African 'bush', among pre-technological people, I came to realise that since their ability to control their environment was limited to a few simple tools, they had to rely upon another resource, namely, the spiritual. So prayers and offerings to God, to the spirit world, to their ancestors was their major 'tool'. In our own technological society we have little or no inclination to turn to supernatural forces to fulfil our needs — except perhaps for the quick prayer in desperation: 'O God, find me a parking space' or the naive assumption that a prayer for fine weather for the following day's picnic will cause God to intervene in the processes of nature! In the words of Dietrich Bonhoeffer, written in prison in 1944: 'Man has learnt to deal with himself in all questions of importance without recourse to the "working hypothesis" called

73

"God". "God" is being pushed more and more out of life, losing more and more ground'.

I consider 6th August 1945 to be the day of a momentous leap forward in humanity's technological control. That day, when the first Atomic Bomb was dropped on Hiroshima, killing 75,000 people and injuring tens of thousands of others, was the first step along the path to various nations building up their stock of nuclear explosives, enough to destroy our planet several times over. Previous to 1945 humanity had been very and horribly ingenious in exterminating hundreds of people at a time or in destroying large areas of vegetation. But that August our capability shifted from mass homicide to omnicide: we took upon ourselves the power to wipe out all life on Earth if not actually to obliterate the planet altogether. We humans took on the role that had previously been regarded as God's alone. To this extent we became as God. We became co-creators in our ability to decide not to obliterate our planet but to maintain it in existence.

The belief that we have reached a critical phase in human history, another Axial Period, has been the subject of a number of recent books. For instance, in *Visions* (1998) by Michio Kaku, a theoretical physicist in New York, the author claims that we have now reached 'the age of mastery'. This has come about, he says, because of three scientific revolutions in recent years: the quantum revolution unlocked the secrets of the atom, the DNA revolution unravelled the molecules of life and the computer has revolutionised the accumulation and dissemination of knowledge. He believes the 21st century will be typified by the cross-fertilisation of these three revolutions.

The other illustration of our taking more charge of our lives is seen in the world-wide movement towards democracy. For a variety of reasons, among which are mass education, the information explosion and the persuasive power of the mass-media, people are no longer content for those higher up the hierarchical ladder — whether in politics or in religion — to tell them how they must act, in what they must believe, how they are to go about their daily lives. The rise of 'people power', the collective power of people at the bottom of the social pile, and their ability to topple dictators and to overthrow repressive regimes, is a feature of our present times. People today want to be in control of their own lives and to have a say in the future they want for their children.

The development of the human sciences: Anthropology (about our origins), Psychology (about how we use our minds) and Sociology (about how we relate to each other) have provided us over the last century with a new level of understanding of our world and of our place in it. More recently we can add Cosmology to the list, by which I mean our story of the birth, the development and the destiny of the Universe which enables us to make sense of our lives, to put our lives in a context. Recent rethinking of this story is causing us to take quite a new position vis-a-vis our place in and our relationship to our world.

And that brings us to what I suggest is another major factor contributing to our present evolutionary leap.

A NEW COSMOLOGY

In proportion to our probing further and further into the Universe, our minds have been expanding concerning our place in it. It was not that long ago in human history that our ancestors were forced to move from the comfortable position of regarding Planet Earth and humanity in particular, not only as the geographic centre of the Universe but as the crown, the pinnacle of creation. They had indeed to make a 'paradigm shift' from believing that all else was created solely for our benefit, or rather, what God wanted above all was creatures who would reflect himself — which could only be us human beings, of course.

Thus we put ourselves above and outside the rest of creation: superior to it. We believed that we existed *on* a planet rather than being one with it. Although our knowledge of the Universe has changed, in reality our Western economics, laws and ethics are still based upon this position of superiority. Morality, until very recently, has been concerned almost entirely with our behaviour towards God and other people, while our treatment of Earth has not been considered to be a moral issue.

Today, as we discover galaxies beyond galaxies we realise that this idea is the ultimate arrogance. Looking out now from our tiny place in the Universe we are faced with the truth that Earth is just one rather small planet among the nine of our Solar System which revolve around one star (our sun) which in turn is just one of a hundred billion stars (or suns) in our galaxy, the Milky Way, which is only one of possibly a hundred billion other galaxies. Even if we could travel at the speed of light — 186,000 miles per second — it would take 100,000 years to travel from one side of our Milky Way galaxy to the other. It is no exaggeration to say that if Planet Earth were the size of a grain of sand on an English beach our nearest star on that scale would be a grain of sand on a beach in Australia. That star, named *Proxima Centauri*, is 23.52 million million miles away.

We are familiar with the Pole Star (Polaris) in the Little Bear constellation. It is so-called because it hovers over our North Pole and for centuries has been a navigational guide to seafarers. It is 500 light-years away.

If we can catch a glimpse of it in a clear sky tonight, we will be looking back into history. We are seeing it as it was 500 years ago!

Recently astronomers caught sight of a super-nova, a star exploding in a far-away galaxy. Not while it was exploding but ten billion years after it had exploded! It had exploded only five billion years after the Big Bang but the light from that event has only now reached us in the Milky Way galaxy. The vastness of the Universe is way beyond our imagining. That is the contribution to our knowledge made by Astrophysics and Astronomy.

But within the realm of Planet Earth we are appreciating more the interconnectedness of all life. There is no one form of life — human life, for instance — that stands superior to or independent of any other form of life. Every element of life contributes to every other. None is a receiver without also being a giver. The newly developed science of Ecology is causing us human beings to re-assess our position within creation. It is causing us to shift from thinking *about* the Planet, to thinking *as* the Planet, as one with it.

Not one of these five phenomena, — the millennium factor, the spiritual experience factor, the population-communications factor, our human adulthood, the new cosmology — taken separately, can be said to be the cause of the evolutionary shift in consciousness that is taking place just now. But all are inter-connected so that together they create a dynamic energy that can be regarded as being a major factor bringing about 'The New'.

The blob picture revealed.
(Pictures reproduced by permission of Dr. Rupert Sheldrake.)

4

CHRISTIANITY CHALLENGED BY THE NEW ERA

The Christian way of life as expressed by different Churches, is not in touch with the culture of our times. So we cannot be surprised that in the western world, the womb of Christianity, the Churches find themselves challenged: even in crisis. Signs of this crisis are the devaluing of their authority, their unsuccessful outreach, their tenuous relations with science, their uncertainty about newly-arising ethical problems, their hesitancy over declarations on sex issues, their falling membership, their ambivalence about the role of women, their unrelated-to-life liturgy and symbolism, their caution about dialogue with other religions, and so on. Take, for example, the continued use by the Churches of a language which has become quite outdated. I am not referring only to the use of the King James Bible or even to the words of some of our Victorian hymns, nor to the 'thee' and 'thy' words, all of which belong to a previous culture than our own. But I refer to the language of a super-natural faith. Take the word 'grace'. Ask any church-goer if she knows the meaning of the word and she will answer 'of course'. But does she? Has she ever stopped to consider what it might mean? For the non-Christian it means 'elegance'.

Can we identify one particular problem that underlies all these symptoms? I believe we can.

I propose that the key problem facing Christianity in western society today is that the Church has become turned in upon itself and forgetful that, in the words of Pope John Paul II: 'The Church is not an end unto itself, since it is ordered towards the Kingdom of God of which it is the seed, the sign and the instrument' *(Redemptoris Missio N.18)*. Christian life has become Church-oriented instead of being Kingdom-oriented.

In calling this a "key problem" I understand it as the Master Key which, when this problem is faced, will open all doors. I am more than ever convinced that the crisis the western Church faces today — and I speak of the Church as the whole Christian community, not simply its leadership — could be addressed in quite a different perspective if this problem were to be faced. This is the Master Key which will enable a new blossoming of Christianity in our New Era.

With the centre of gravity having moved away from the new world order which Jesus came to reveal to us in terms of the Kingdom or Reign of God, towards Church concerns, the shift has also been away from nourishing that element of our humanity which we call 'Spirituality', towards concern with its outward, collective expression which we label 'Religion'. (We made the important distinction between Spirituality and Religion in the last chapter.) For many today their church is no more than a Worship Centre.

ORTHODOXY OR ORTHOPRAXIS

With the emphasis within Christianity upon religion there has become a greater concern about what Church members believe than about the quality of their lives.

Lists of beliefs — Creeds — have become the check list to determine whether an individual belongs or not. This has become so important a pass to membership that both the Catholic and Anglican communions teach that there are 'truths necessary for salvation'.

It is curious that the Christian religion is the exception in being more concerned with what its followers believe (orthodoxy) than with the way they live (orthopraxis). Surely, the only purpose for which we pass this period of our lives on Planet Earth is to grow in love. This is the only thing God wants of us, and it has to be given in freedom. God does not require our knowledge: He[1] has enough of that! So why this insistence on right believing, especially since Jesus himself indicated that it was the way we love that would be a mark of our discipleship? 'If you have love for one another, then everyone will know that you are my disciples' (John.13:35). So why this insistence on right believing? Knowledge of matters divine is no more than a means to an end: to enable us to become more loving people. I think of the words: 'You were taught the truth that is *in* Jesus' (Ephesians 5:2), which seems to me to translate Jesus' own words, speaking as the Christ: 'I am the way, the truth and the life' (John14:6), which we can paraphrase as: 'Truth, as I live it, is the Way to Life'.

Could an explanation be that while the other major religions are more closely related to a culture (Jews, Arabs, Indians, Chinese, Japanese, Tibetans) which provides their unifying element, Christianity being world-wide and not tied to any particular culture, has only one way of assessing who belongs and who does not: by requiring members to tick their assent to a list of doctrines?

---

1 Throughout this book I shall use a capital 'H' with He, Him, as pronouns for God as distinct from a gendered he, or she.

I am not the first to say that Christianity has to move — or move back — from a religion of doctrines to a religion of relationships. As a friend of mine recently expressed it: 'We are coming to recognise that Christianity is neither a system of morality nor a collection of beliefs *about* God, but rather the promise of union *with* God'.

From this there follows another characteristic distinguishing a Church-centred from a Kingdom-centred Christianity. The former is exclusive, people are either inside or outside, members or not. While the Kingdom of God is inclusive, all-embracing. The Kingdom is not something one chooses to join: there is no membership. It is the Divine intention being worked out in our space-time dimension, in which the whole of creation is involved, whether aware of it or not.

We can summarise the differences thus:

KINGDOM	CHURCH
Spirituality	Religion
Loving relationships	Assent to beliefs
Inclusive	Exclusive

Spirituality unites people; religion divides. Those of us who answer to the name 'Christian' because we believe that the historical, fully aware, person of Jesus is the ultimate Christ, the most supreme manifestation of the Divine possible within the limitations of a human person, must believe also that it is his message to humanity which addresses, in the most complete way possible, the problems we face in living in our inharm-onious world.

THE JESUS MESSAGE

His message is encapsulated in the first place in the manner of his own way of living and dying. It was expressed, secondly, in what he said which was the explanation he offered of the ideal, the vision, which inspired his life. The core of that message, which he referred to as Good News, he spoke of in terms of the Kingdom or Reign of God. Andrew Harvey writes *(Son of Man):*

> 'Paying attention to how Jesus acted and in what context and to what he really said — and not to the dogmas surrounding his divinity — can have the paradoxical effect of making us take him and his words even more seriously and, above all, in the highest and most urgent sense, practically'.

Christianity is not a new ethic. It is a new life which brings us into direct contact with God. This must be our starting point because it is a vision coming to birth out of the reality of a life lived on Earth. There is no divine truth that reaches us from anywhere outside our Universe. We have to discover truth — in this case God's purpose for creation — from within creation itself. As Thomas Berry, the cultural historian and theologian, has said: 'The Universe itself, but especially Planet Earth, needs to be experienced as the primary mode of divine presence' *(The Dream of the Earth)* and consequently the only source of anything we can know about God. So he calls the Universe 'the primary religious reality .... the primary revelation of the divine'.

When as a small boy I started to learn the Catechism (by heart!) I was told that we were 'made in the image and likeness of God'. The implication of this statement is that we already know all about God and could therefore interpret our humanity in that perspective. Needless to say this upside-down approach did not worry me as a child, but it does as an adult. Our starting point can be none other than the knowledge we have of our humanity through our experience and from this we build an image of what we call divine and a vision of what the end or *telos* of creation is: God's intent.

The kind of God that the Church continues to preach about, declare in its Creeds, offer reverence and praise to, sing hymns about and implore in its prayers, is incompatible with most peoples' everyday experience living in a world that is going through a scientific and technological revolution. Today's world is culturally so entirely different from the biblical world, a world that in all other respects exists in museums and history books, that the answers the Church continues to offer to humanity's fundamental questions about life — that gave rise to our need for religion in the first place — are on a different wavelength from the form those questions take today. Yet the very development of our science and technology and the consequential loss of our sense of the transcendent, makes it more imperative than ever that we develop the spiritual dimension of our lives if we are to maintain our sanity as human beings.

We can never know God as God; we can only work with images. "God" is the name we give to the Reality that is beyond all names. Different cultures have created their own images which answer best to their spiritual needs. While the Hindus express their understanding of God in a range of images — elephant, monkey, Vishnu — Moslems forbid all images, paintings, icons, symbols of God. But both are saying the same: God cannot be perceived in totality by the human mind. So Hindus approach God through innumerable partial aspects of the divine, Moslems by admitting shere transcendence.

Both the Romans and the Greeks had their pantheons — their temples dedicated to all their gods - but the latter admitted the limitation of this display with their 'altar to an Unknown God' (Acts.17:23). The Jews of Jesus' time realised that God was so 'other' that they would not so much as pronounce his name which had previously been written in the Hebrew Scriptures as YHWH (Yahweh) but said instead Adonai which can be translated as 'Lord'.

Up to present times there have been two diametrically opposed ways of perceiving the Ultimate Reality, in the world's religions:

WESTERN	EASTERN
Super-nature Theism	*Pan-Theism*
God resides above	All that is, is God
and outside creation	There is nothing beyond
A transcendent God	An immanent God

which in many ways still pertain, but as we shall see, today many people's ideas are crossing frontiers.

The long theological tradition of the West, initially born in the Jewish tradition, then developed as Christianity, Islam and the Bahai, has been what I am calling "Supernature Theism". God the creator is a being distinct from the natural, from creation, watching over it, sustaining it, empowering it, ruling over it and even, until the last couple of centuries ago, popularly regarded to be dwelling "up there" in Heaven, above creation.

Xenophanes, a Greek philosopher (500BCE) attacking the immoral behaviour of the gods as portrayed by Homer and Hesiod, commented sarcastically:

> Human beings think of the gods as having been born, wearing clothes, speaking and having bodies like their own. Ethiopians say the gods are black with snub noses. Thracians say they have blue eyes and red hair. If cows and horses had hands they would draw pictures of the gods looking like cows and horses.

And still today we Western people project God as a super-human being because we know of nothing more sublime. Our naming and notion of God are our human creation. Each culture created an image of God such that it made them feel superior to all other cultures. The Hebrews, for instance, believed a male God would fight

85

their battles for them because He hated the enemies which they hated.

The Christian God evolved from these roots and the image of God as being super-nature is with us still. However at the time of Jesus the Hebrew God was so remote, majestic and transcendent that His name could not even be uttered. To do so was blasphemy. When Jesus brought Him down to our level by addressing Him as an intimate father, he gave us a personalised God. The Church went further, centuries later, by trinitising God, but in doing so has got us entangled with the image of 'persons'. With this personalised God and Jesus' father-God, Christians are stuck with an image, an idol, of a God who is super-human-sized. It becomes idolatry when the image is taken for the reality instead of being accepted as an inadequate glimpse of Ultimate Reality beyond our comprehension.

The diametrically opposite image of God is non-personal. It is that found in the major eastern religions. Take Buddhism, for example. Buddhists simply do not think of the Divinity as an external deity. Their way of thinking of God is so different from ours that some Christians are under the impression that Buddhists are atheists! If they were to do it at all, Buddhists would address the question WHAT is God, not WHO is God. For them, all that is, is God.

A RELEVANT GOD

I suggest that for us today, for whom an external, above-nature, male God is becoming a less and less attractive image in the light of our explaining reality in the language of Quantum Physics, and with our expanding knowledge of the vastness of the Universe, we can, nevertheless, perceive God in terms which are to be found in the Bible:

wind, spirit which brooded over chaos in the story of creation. God as *life-giver, source of vitality. Love* that deepens our relationships and thereby expands our humanity.

Some theologians today are employing a word which bridges the transcendental and the immanent: *pan-en-theism*. God is in everything and everything is in God. While preserving the Western understanding of the Creator and creation being separate, it learns from the East that we have to look inwards, to the very essence of our being, to find God.

To say God is not a Person, even a Super-person, is not to say God is not personal and that I as a person cannot have a personal relationship with God. When we speak of a 'personal God' we do not mean that God is *a* person but that we attribute to God the two supreme faculties of the human person — those which differentiate us from other beings in the animal kingdom — namely, the ability to be self-conscious, in the sense of being able to reflect upon our own consciousness, and the ability to love. We say God is all-knowing, meaning God is Supreme Consciousness. Or, to put it the other way about, Supreme, Ultimate Consciousness is God. Ultimate Consciousness (Truth) is the epitome of all knowing. The purest and highest form of Energy is Love. God is Love (1 John 4:8). God is Energy, the continually-creating energy. But God is not that which is the product of this energy. God is that energy which gives continued existence to every planet, every star, every galaxy and maybe to other universes. There is as much God-energy in the furthest star we can know about as there is in Planet Earth. It is cosmic-size. But in saying this we are not defining God, we are only giving a new expression to the Ultimate Reality within our limitations as Earthlings. To say we have to look inwards to our experience of energy, of life, of love, to know God, rather than outward and above creation, is to pursue a line of thought that matches better our understanding of all else in life today.

To shift our perception of God is the fundamental task that will enable the present-day Church with its Kingdom Good News to touch present-day people. This is why our reference point must be the historical person of Jesus. Whatever myths surround the story of his birth, whatever interpretations we give to his appearances after his death, our concern must be with the message he gave us: in sum, the Reign of God. 'I must preach the Good News of the Kingdom of God .... because that is what God sent me to do' (Luke 4:43).

The kernel of that Good News was that life need not be like it is. Things can be different. It stirred in his listeners that deepest of human aspirations, to reach out for 'the better'. Why do any of us feel prompted to attempt anything new, except that we believe good, the better-than-now will come of it? Every human heart is drawn towards 'more'. At a gross level this is understood as having more — possessions, power, popularity — but in its more refined state it is about being more. That is, we long to grow, to achieve, to overcome our personal barriers and inhibitions — to be more. The energy that draws us is our fundamental attraction towards our ultimate fulfilment. 'My soul is restless till it rests in thee,' said St Augustine. Nothing gives us a greater sense of well-being than to realise that we have 'grown' in this latter sense. It is this that is the basis of spirituality — as different from religion — the attraction towards our higher self.

The Good News for today, as it has always been, is that this journey towards our fulfilment is a possibility. It is the fundamental teaching of every religion, each differing only in the path it proposes. What touched the hearts of Jesus' audience as new was that the good he proposed was achievable. The path to bliss was not by keeping the 365 regulations that the religious leaders had imposed upon the Jewish people, but by living their relationships differently: a relationship of familiarity with their God and a treating of their fellow humans as brothers and sisters. In their own eyes his audience were nobodies and he called them to become somebodies — they were valued, they mattered. The only way they could experience this was by seeing that they mattered to those around them. That they were valued by God was a theory: that they mattered to their neighbour was an experience. All else labelled 'religion' had to be subordinate to that, a means to that end.

The Good News that people should be hearing from the Church today, as the contemporary voice of Jesus, is the same. But with this difference, that to touch people as both 'news' and 'good' it must be expressed in today's language as fulfilling their deepest longings as they experience these longings at this moment in history.

The late Pedro Arrupe, the influential Superior General of the Jesuits said already in the early 1980s:

> I'm afraid that we are about to offer yesterday's answers to address tomorrow's problems, that we are talking in such a way that people no longer understand us, that we are using a language that doesn't go to the heart of men and women. If that's the case, then we'll talk a great deal, but only to ourselves. In fact no one will be listening to us any more, because no one will grasp what we're trying to say.

I end this chapter with a quotation from Albert Schweitzer:

> Christianity can only become the living truth for successive generations if thinkers constantly arise within it who, in the spirit of Jesus, make belief in him capable of intellectual apprehension in the thought forms of the world-view proper to their times. *(The Mysticism of Paul the Apostle)*

In Part Two we will try to unravel the meaning of the 'Kingdom' message of Jesus; the way in which he presented his understanding of God's vision for creation.

PART TWO

Unravelling the Vision of Jesus

"The Kingdom of God movement was Jesus' programme of empowerment for a peasantry steadily more hard-pressed, in that first-century Jewish homeland, through insistent taxation, attendant indebtedness and eventual land expropriation, all within increasing commercialisation in the booming colonial economy of a Roman Empire under Augustan peace and a Lower Galilee under Herodian urbanisation. Jesus lived, against the systemic injustice and structural evil of that situation, an alternative open to all who would accept it: a life of open healing and shared eating, of radical itinerancy and fundamental egalitarianism, of human contact without discrimination and divine contact without hierarchy. That, he said, was how God would run the world if God, not Caesar, sat on its imperial throne."

— Dominic John Crossan
Who Killed Jesus?

5

THE VISION

There was a man who lived in the Middle East some two thousand years ago who had a vision of how our world might be. We do not know that he said much about our relationship to Mother Earth, probably believing that if we got two other dimensions of our relationships right, everything else would fall into place. The vision he shared with anyone who would listen was about living with a quite new way of relating to each other and relating to God.

He was a Jew living in Palestine and his name was Jesus. Today he is usually referred to as 'Jesus Christ'. This is not a double-barrelled name but a name and a title. He is Jesus the Christ. St Paul writes: 'The Christ is the visible likeness of the invisible God' (Colossians 1:15). The Christ existed timelessly before creation — the 'Word' spoken of in the prologue to John's gospel — while Jesus was born in Earth's time. Jesus was a Jew: Christ is not. Christians believe that Jesus was the greatest embodiment of a Spirit-filled person, the most perfect manifestation of the Christ that human limitations allow. To say Jesus is the Christ is not the same as to say the Christ is Jesus. As we go back to the sources available to us, the writings of the New Testament, we need to bear in mind not what Jesus has become through Christian tradition, but what he himself claimed to be — or rather, did not claim to be. In the words of the theologians, the two brothers Hanson, (in their book *Reasonable Belief*) 'On the basis of the evidence available we must conclude that Jesus did not teach that he was God, did not claim to be God, did not believe that he was God'. We often find him praying to God.

Considering the influence he has had on western civilisation for two thousand years, it is astonishing we know so little about him as historical fact. There is nothing every Christian would wish more than to be able to read a biography of Jesus. We expect biographies to tell us all about the person, their appearance, their personality, their strong and their weak points as well as a chronological record of their lives.

But in the four gospels we have none of that. They are not, and they were never meant to be, biographical. They were not written like a diary at the time of Jesus' life. Luke tells us (3:23) he was *about* thirty years old when he began his public ministry, but the Greek phrasing could mean that he was any age between, let us say, twenty-eight and thirty-two. Mark makes it look as though Jesus completed everything in one year, while John's account requires at least three years — which is the common tradition — because of the number of major festivals mentioned. G.H.Streeter, a New Testament scholar, tells us that apart from the forty days Jesus reportedly spent in the desert — and the number forty is frequently used symbolically in the Hebrew Scriptures to signify a period of preparation — everything reported to have been said or done by Jesus in all four gospels would have occupied less than three weeks.

Mark's gospel was probably the earliest of the four and was written some thirty-five years after the crucifixion. Luke's came next, borrowing heavily from Mark and then came Matthew who borrowed from both. John's gospel came much later, probably around the year 100. Biblical scholars think it likely that there were already some earlier texts written, but now lost, upon which the evangelists drew. It is supposed that there was one (designated 'Q', a shorthand for *Quelle* which means 'source' in German) being a collection of the sayings of Jesus. Each Gospel was written for a particular readership to give those people what the writer felt they ought to know about the 'Good News' of Jesus.

In contemporary terms we can regard the evangelists as Jesus' 'spin-doctors'. Good spin-doctors do not falsify the truth but they put a particular spin on their announcements so as to show up their hero or his policy in the best possible light in relation to a particular audience.

Since the gospels are not accounts of what exactly happened, we can understand why we find apparent contradictions. The writers were less concerned about historical facts than about the spiritual meaning behind them. *(See chart page 98).*

Because the New Testament opens with the four Gospels most Christians presume that they were not only written in the Matthew, Mark, Luke, John order but that they were written before all the other books that follow. This is not so. Most of the letters attributed to St Paul are the earliest texts of the New Testament. This is an important point. St Paul wrote letters to Christian communities that already existed, that were already attracted by the Good News of Jesus, or at least what

Writers of Chronicles

A cultural, as much as a linguistic, "translation" is required to appreciate fully what the New Testament contains.

	Contemporary writers of history	**New Testament writers**
Purpose:	To transmit facts	To proclaim an experience
Truth:	Objective Factually correct	Subjective To serve the explanation of an experience
Chronology:	Important Substantiates facts	Quite unimportant Serves the proclamation
Content:	Myth has no place	Tradition, liturgy, myth add weight to experience
Prophecy:	Only a "fancy that" factor, post-event	Prophecy gives authenticity. Facts will be bent accordingly
Contradictions:	A challenge	An irrelevance

they had heard of this Good News according to St Paul's interpretation of it. (We must remember that he was not an eye-witness to the life of Jesus and that he learnt about Jesus from those that were. So St Paul's message is already second-hand [1.Corinthians 15:3]).

For all the above reasons we cannot be sure that we have an accurate account of almost any of the reported words of Jesus nor of many of the events. In fact we can be sure that we have very little record of what actually occurred and what was actually said, although we may believe that something along the lines of what is reported occurred. This is why we have to admit that the Gospels are a product of the memory, reflections and experiences of the early Christian communities. By the time the Gospels were written, the new Jesus movement had parted from its Jewish roots and begun to structure itself into a new religion with its own form of worship. Yet it is apparent that Jesus never intended to found a new religion, he gave us no rubrics for worship, he did not ordain any priests to lead the liturgy nor give us any dogmatic definitions. All these have emerged as the new communities became more structured.

Gregory J. Riley writes *(One Jesus, Many Christs):*

> Jesus was what scholars in the field of religion call a "master figure", and master figures never fit in with the traditions from which they come. They are rare geniuses who are in conflict with their own religious inheritance and by their creative spirituality are able to set a whole culture on some new path.
>
> Something about him [Jesus] forever changed not only the Judaisms of his day, but all subsequent western religious understanding.

His vision is still revolutionary by today's values which is why, perhaps, after two thousand years, despite the power exercised world-wide in his name, the thrust of his message has been misunderstood, softened-down, forgotten, ignored, distorted or dismissed. Yet those who call themselves his followers believe that the only hope for the future of our planet is to take his message seriously and make his vision our own.

HOW DID JESUS ARRIVE AT HIS VISION ?

Can we trace the cultural influences which sparked off that energy that drove him to realise, in his own person and among those around him, the vision of a society ordered by an interior, spiritual power, rather than that in which he lived, controlled by external, human, political power? What was the dynamic of his sense of mission?

There would seem to be two factors which contributed to this. The first is the beliefs which had been assumed into Hebrew theology from the Zoroastrian religion during the Jews' forty-eight years in exile in Babylon, and secondly, the grip that apocalyptic ideas had on Jesus' contemporaries.

But before we unpack these two factors, a word needs to be said about the knowledge and wisdom that Jesus acquired. I say 'acquired' deliberately because, however much Jesus lived in Christ-consciousness, he had no other way of acquiring knowledge than the two ways that are the channel of knowledge for all of us human beings. The first is that knowledge which we call 'rational knowledge' because it is received from outside us, through our five senses of sight, hearing, smell, taste and touch, and is then 'rationalised' by the brain. In other words it is 'processed': linked with previous knowledge and stored away in the memory. This type of knowledge bears the stamp of our upbringing, our culture, our education, our religion, our experience, from what we read or hear or see.

There is also an inner source of knowledge, more often referred to as Wisdom, which comes to us from within, intuitively, inspired by and triggered by goodness-knows what! The very word 'in-tuition' is instructive: it is tuition from within. Such knowledge bears no relationship to our level of education or degree of experience, or age or religious background, although it does bear on these when our rational mind comes to interpret our intuition. The sages, the wise people of our history, have a great capacity for this inner wisdom, which, we might say, is a God-given gift, offered to every person open to receive it. We meet this distinction in the Letter to the Ephesians (3:19): 'Know (wisdom) the love of Christ which surpasses (rational) knowledge'.

Jesus would have built up his intellectual reservoir from both sources. His rational knowledge would have been sourced from the social and religious culture in which he was raised as a child, from what he learned from his parents, from the local Rabbi and from his weekly attendance at synagogue. But as a 'sage', an enlightened human being, conscious of his union with God, his intuitive faculty would have been developed to the highest degree.

JESUS' EXPERIENCE OF GOD

Jesus clearly experienced a close relationship with God which was unique, indeed quite at variance with his own culture and religion. While his fellow Jews held God at a distance, with such awe that they would not even pronounce the divine name, Jesus felt and spoke of an intimacy with the Divine such that he addressed God as *Abba*, Dad. What was the experience that moved Jesus from Yahweh to Abba? We can only speculate. He must have felt in Joseph a father who was protective, nurturing, teaching and secure. It has traditionally been supposed that Joseph died not long after Jesus was twelve years old because no further mention is made of him. Did Jesus' experience of closeness to God replace the father of his boyhood? God was a presence for him 'as if a father'. But we notice too that Jesus liked to pray to God in the open, on a hill-top, in silence, and sometimes through the night, under the stars, experiencing God also in the immensity of the Universe.

VISION OF A NEW BEGINNING

So to return to our question: what sparked off Jesus' zeal for bringing about the sort of world he understood God wanted? While being empowered by wisdom, the manner in which he communicated his vision would necessarily have been drawn on his cultural upbringing, that of a first century Jew. That is not to say that he did not experience being God-directed, but the picture of the kind of world he wanted to see realised would be in the context of his times and his Jewish culture.

We cannot comment on the wisdom component, but we can on the rational component. When the Jews were banished, exiled in Babylon for two generations — from 587 to 539 BCE — they naturally absorbed a number of traditions from the culture in which they were immersed which was influenced by the teaching of the Persian prophet Zoroaster (Zarathustra). In Zoroaster's understanding the world was not static but moving, through conflict, towards a consummation which would result in a perfect conflict-free state. From this concept we can find a number of elements appearing in Jewish belief (and eventually into Christian belief), not found among the Jews before the Exile. Among these are the forecast of a cosmic conflict in which the forces of evil will be finally overthrown, the idea of angels, a personal devil and accompanying demons, the recording of our deeds in a Book of Life, the separation of the body and soul at death, a general resurrection and universal judgement with an after-life of reward or punishment and the vision of a messianic figure who would introduce a new age by overthrowing the powers of evil. (Incidentally, if you think it is only religious beliefs that our present western culture inherited from the Babylonians, have a look at your watch: it was they who based the counting of time and the measuring of angles on the number 60!)

The second factor that would seem to have contributed to Jesus' vision was contemporary. Apocalyptic literature was very widespread among the Jews of his time (and later among the early Christians) offering visions and revelations of the future and other divine mysteries. One form of this with which we are probably familiar is the last book of the Bible, the Book of Revelation, in some bibles called The Apocalypse. The term 'apocalyptic' refers to that religious outlook which contrasts the present time of suffering with a new age which will be joyful and eternal. It will suddenly break in from outside by divine intervention. In the word's of Mary's *Magnificat:* 'He has pulled down the mighty from their thrones' (Luke 1:52) which echoes I Samuel 2:10, 'The enemies of Yahweh are shattered, the Most High thunders in the heavens'. We find these apocalyptic views expressed by Jesus (in Mark 13, Matthew 24, Luke 21) or were they perhaps put into the mouth of Jesus by the gospel writers living at a time when apocalyptic thought was prevalent, as is clearly seen in the earliest of St Paul's letters (I Thessalonians 4 and 5)? These views have been associated with the Christian belief in the Second Coming, expressed in the words of the Creed: 'He will come again in glory to judge the living and the dead, and his kingdom will have no end'.

Curiously, the description given in Peter's epistle of the end of time is extraordinarily like that given by astronomers today forecasting the time when the energy of our Sun will eventually be exhausted and become a great expanding ball of fire which will burn up everything on Planet Earth and destroy all life: 'The day of the Lord will come like a thief, and then with a roar the sky will vanish, the heavenly bodies will burn up and be destroyed, the Earth and all it contains will vanish' (II Peter 3:10). The author believed this cataclysm was just around the corner: today we calculate our Sun still has four and a half billion years of life left!

Just as the Christian apocalypses flourished during the Roman persecution of the new religion, the Jewish apocalypses were written to bring hope and comfort to the Jews suffering the domination of first the Greeks and then the Romans. Jesus lived in this cultural context and within it he expressed his message. He reflected the beliefs of his day that the end time was immanent. He was not only a prophet but probably regarded himself as the last of the prophets. 'I tell you there are some here who will not die until they have seen the Kingdom of God come with power' (Mark 9:1) and 'Remember that all these things will happen before the people now living have all died' (Matthew 24:34). In one of his earlier books *The World to Come*, Don Cupitt writes:

> Jesus vigorously proclaimed the end of the world and the coming of a new era in which religion would cease to be a burdensome external demand and would become instead an inner spirit of liberty. Mankind would come of age and a new humanity would be born.

Although, just when this was to come about, Jesus claimed ignorance (Matthew 24:36). Was it because Jesus foresaw 'the end was nigh' that he did not launch a new religion and did not offer any alternative to the social, political or economic structures of his time? If he believed he was living at the end of human history, did he even intend to found a community — today's Church — to continue his mission? Many scholars today regard the birth of the Church as a community of continuing mission to be a development from the preaching of St Paul who later came to realise that the Second Coming was not to be as imminent as he first thought, and as he had expressed in his earliest letter (I Thessalonians 4:15-18).

PRESENTING THE VISION

Since Jesus was sharing his vision far more with the 'ordinary' people, the peasantry, than with the elite, he had to speak of it in their terms, in imagery. He had to give his vision a name and a name which would grab their imagination. Being a man of his time, of his culture, of his religious background, he referred to the perfect world as he envisioned it as a kingdom. The 'Kingdom of God' he called it.

But in naming it he also took a risk. It had to be a name which his listeners could latch onto because it would not be entirely strange to them. The notion of a Kingdom of God featured in their tradition. On the other hand he did not intend to describe a national territory, as their tradition meant, but a spiritual experience. So he took the risk of being misunderstood. And he was, both by those who felt threatened by it (John. 18:33) and even by his closest followers (Acts 1:6). (A more appropriate

103

expression is the 'reign' of God, but because our Scripture uses the term 'Kingdom', we will keep to that here.)

Because Jesus was proposing an experience of a new way of living, with new values, we do not find in any of the records of what he said that he ever defined it. How can one define an experience? The best we can do to understand his meaning is to piece together a number of clues found in his actions and words and so form a composite picture.

JESUS' VISION IN TERMS OF A KINGDOM

In today's literature on the subject, one meets various attempts to create this composite picture.

Perhaps the least dramatic, echoing what we find in the Letter to the Ephesians, is: *'The world the way God meant it to be'*. Thinking of the Kingdom as the final stage of human evolution, one author defined it as simply: *'A higher state of consciousness'*. Another amplifies that concept: *'A situation in which life is ordered by interior, spiritual power rather than by external, human-controlled power'*.

Jesus reflected this vision in his very being. This was possible because he lived in this higher state of consciousness. Although as a child and an adolescent he had to go through a process of learning facts and skills, as all of us have had to do, parallel with his physical growth, he was, from his earliest years of self-awareness, also growing in a state of Unity Consciousness, so that by the end of his life he could tell his closest friends: 'I am in the Father and the Father is in me' (John 14:10). On account of this he was freed from those inhibitions induced by fear that we suffer: our concern for self-preservation, our struggle to rise above a situation, our longing to be recognised, to be liked, to be loved.

104

His union, immediacy with God in Unity Consciousness, resulted in his having no fear to be completely human. He accepted his humanity as sheer gift: his identity as an expression of divine, total love. The certainty he enjoyed of being loved accounted for his authority to live and speak as he did. He was not intimidated by a fear of risk-taking. He was fully 'his own man'. He projected himself from a solid foundation, a complete self-assurance, a secure depth.

The prayer of Jesus at the Last Supper was that all humanity should share his state of Unity Consciousness (John.14), or, as it is sometimes called, Christ Consciousness, which means living and acting from the consciousness of how much we too are Christs. St Paul tells us we are Christ-filled: 'God's plan is to make known his secret to his people, this rich and glorious secret, which he has for all peoples. And the secret is that Christ is in you' (Colossians 1:27). And he says of himself: 'It is no longer I who live, but it is the Christ who lives in me' (Galatians 2:20).

Since the source of the creative energy to make the Kingdom a reality is God, it is not through our activity or achievement at a surface level that it is going to become a reality but by more of us living in and acting out of a deeper state of consciousness. In this way we become a channel of God's energy, allowing God to achieve His vision through us. By such co-operation with the Divine Will we become co-creators of the New Kingdom Era.

When Jesus tells Pilate 'My Kingdom is not of this world' he is not implying that it is on another planet but rather that it exists in another dimension of consciousness.

The theologian John Macquarrie in his *Principles of Christian Theology* describes the Kingdom as that *'Commonwealth of free beings, united in Being and with each other through love'* and this is echoed by another writer in a more simple form: *'God's vision is for all humanity to live in harmony together and with the whole of Creation'*. And in an even briefer form yet: *'A new way of living relationships'*.

We should not be dismissive of the brevity of some of the above descriptions. They are charged with meaning as we will be able to appreciate if we explore a little further how entirely new and all-embracing was the vision Jesus called the Kingdom of God.

John's gospel has Jesus speak of it in terms of 'the fullness of life' (10:10). Another way of expressing this is to say that it addresses every person's deepest human desire to grow, to be more. This can be achieved by everyone only in a perfect society. The Kingdom is the expression of that perfect society, 'ordered by interior spiritual power', not of a society of material values.

We human beings are already raised to a higher Kingdom than the Animal Kingdom. But we cannot speak of a Human Kingdom as beneath or lower than the Divine Kingdom, or Kingdom of God. That by which we are human is that by which we are divine. To say that the Divine Plan is the sanctification of humanity means our coming to awareness of the presence of the Divine within us. This is what it means to enter, to make the break-through into, the Kingdom of God; not by a deeper understanding, at the cerebral level, but in our manner of loving, of living, of relating, of serving.

JESUS' PROCLAMATION

It is often forgotten that Jesus did not preach about himself, nor about the Church nor even explicitly about God. He spoke about the intention God had in creating our world in all its perfection and of how to bring that about. It was God's 'plan' for the world from the beginning of time. He spoke of 'The Kingdom which has been prepared for you since the creation of the world' (Matthew 25:34). Consequently it is a mistake to say, as many theologians and Church documents often do, that Jesus 'inaugurated' the Kingdom of God. He did not inaugurate it. He was conscious of it, he translated that consciousness into the values by which he lived and thereby manifested the possibility of this vision becoming a reality.

FROM UTOPIA TO TOPIA

Jesus himself was a living manifestation of the vision. And in living the vision it moved from a possibility, from 'Utopia' (meaning in Greek that which does not anywhere exist) to a reality, a 'Topia' (that which exists somewhere).

Since it is of the essence of our human survival instinct to live with the hope of a 'better tomorrow', our history has seen a succession of Utopias. This is attested to in all cultures and civilisations. We see it in the Epic of Gilgamesh among the Babylonian people, among the Tupi-Guarani Indians of Latin America, in the biblical Book of Revelation (21:4-5). It is expressed in Plato's 'Republic', in Campanella's 'City of Sun', in Kant's 'City of Eternal Peace', in Marx's Proletarian Paradise, in Hegel's Absolute State, in Teilhard de Chardin's Planetisation of Humanity by Love, down to today's several visions of a 'New World Order' including Maharishi's 'Kingdom of Heaven on Earth'.

It was this innate expectation of better-to-come that attracted Jesus' listeners. Contrary to what has often been taught (due to a misunderstanding of use of the expression 'Kingdom of Heaven') that the Kingdom Jesus spoke of was purely spiritual, beyond this world, his subject was

107

the present life and what it could become. This is why it is 'Good News'. He would hardly have been able to enthuse the masses at the bottom of the social pile — those who bore the burden of excessive taxation by the religious leaders on top of what was demanded of them by the Romans — if he had been speaking only of religious observance and the hereafter. He was speaking of the totality of life in this world, spiritual and material. He was concerned with the totality of human life: body, mind and spirit. His acts of physical healing were not just works of wonder, nor demonstrations that he was divine, but 'signs' (as the gospel of John calls them) that a new energy was bursting forth through him which would 'renew the face of the Earth'.

The expectancy of a new political order was widespread at the time of Jesus. The Pharisees, a group of particularly pious laity, believed they could speed up its coming by the faithful and minute observance of all the laws. The Essenes and the monks of Qumran retreated to the desert believing they could bring it about by living a life of legal observance and ascetic purification, while the Zealots believed they could provoke the intervention of God by guerrilla tactics and violence.

Ever since the Jews had returned from their Exile in Babylon, and increasingly in the decades preceding the time of Jesus, the theme of the Kingdom of God was central to their thought. But it possessed a political connotation — self-rule, independence from colonial occupation — because for the Jews politics was one with religion.

So the message of Jesus was not what they were expecting. He did not preach Jewish nationalism, he never spoke a word about rebelling against Rome. Indeed, he implicitly approved of paying the Roman tax (Matthew 22:21). He never referred to restoring the previous glorious kingdom of David, though many understood his message in this way (Mark 11:10) and even his own disciples were expecting it, as was expressed in the disappointment of two of his followers walking to Emmaus after his death: 'We had hoped that he would be the one who was going to set Israel free' (Luke 24:21).

Jesus was speaking about a quality of life: of individuals changing their attitudes (Luke 13:3,5). The liberation he spoke of was in terms of relationships. It was to be a liberation from the burden of legalism, from the oppression of religious rituals and observances, from authoritarianism. Indeed, from an exterior religion to a spiritual awakening. From a hierarchically structured society of social and class privilege to a communitarian society. This is probably why the marginalised more quickly and readily grasped his message than did the elite. They had nothing to lose. He himself did not respect the division of classes. His greater concern was for those who were despised because of their poverty or their mixed blood or their contagious disease or their lowly occupations (Matthew 11:19). He converses with prostitutes, welcomes Gentiles, receives hospitality from a thief (Zaccheus), allows women to accompany him and his male friends. Little wonder the pious were shocked (Matthew 11:19). If everyone were to 'love their neighbour as themselves' as he did with unconditional love, there would be no judging or putting down of others. The distinctions between the pure and the impure would cease to be made.

A VISION FOR TODAY

If the core of Jesus' Kingdom message was about right relationships then the core of that message in turn was about living with the knowledge that one is divine, and recognising the Divine in others with all the consequences of that for oneself and for one's relationships. As one author puts it, Jesus 'gave people back to themselves'. He restored their birthright, their dignity as mirrors of God. Their security was not to be found in the minute observances of the Law, nor in social or religious structures, but in a new consciousness of their personal worth. This is the seed of a personal and global transformation. Recognising the divine presence in oneself, in others and also in all of creation's myriad expressions overcomes the duality by which we in the West live our lives. For as long as human history has been recorded, we have set people apart: them and us, allies and enemies. Even since the United Nations was founded half a century ago our world has suffered from over a hundred and fifty wars. When human consciousness moves into a higher, unitive state the necessity for wars to satisfy our desires will have ceased. This is what is meant by 'Kingdom living'. And by the very living of it we cause it to become a reality already now, in our surroundings.

If we understand what Jesus said about the Kingdom of God as living with a consciousness of God's all-pervading presence, it offers a refreshingly new understanding of the parables. Let us look at two familiar ones in this light.

> The Kingdom of Heaven is like this. A man takes a mustard seed and sows it in his field. It is the smallest of all seeds, but when it grows up, it is the biggest of all plants. It becomes a tree, so that birds come and make their nests in its branches. (Matthew 13:31-32).

Think of the seed as a seed of divine energy planted in the soil of our consciousness. Our consciousness expands as we cultivate it through the practice of deep meditation and service to others. It has the power to transform us and,

110

with us, our surroundings. The Scripture scholar Dominic Crossan tells us in *Jesus: A Revolutionary Biography:*

> The mustard plant is dangerous even when domesticated in the garden and is deadly when growing wild in the grain fields. And those nesting birds, which might strike us as charming, represented to ancient farmers a permanent danger to the seed and grain. The point, in other words, is not just that the mustard plant starts as a proverbially small seed and grows into a shrub of three, four or even more feet in height. It is that it tends to take over where it is not wanted, that it tends to get out of control and it tends to attract birds within cultivated areas, where they are not particularly desired. And that, Jesus said, was what the Kingdom was like.

It becomes a great evolutionary power taking over total life. Again:

> The Kingdom of Heaven is like this. A woman takes some yeast and mixes it with forty litres of flour until the whole batch of dough rises. (Matthew 13:33)

Judaism considered leaven as a symbol of corruption while unleavened bread stood for what is holy. Jesus is turning the accepted values of the world upside-down. The yeast, the divine energy is at work everywhere, not just in those things we human beings choose to call holy. When the Kingdom becomes a reality, when all the dough rises, it will be evident to all.

A COMPLETELY NEW MIND-SET

The earliest announcement of the Kingdom, according to Mark's account, has Jesus saying:

> The right time has come and the Kingdom of God is at hand. Turn away from your sins and believe this Good News! (Mark 1:15)

'Turn away from your sins' is given in some translations as 'repent'. This is often thought to mean 'express

111

sorrow', 'feel guilty', 'do penance'. The gospel texts upon which our translations are based were written in Greek and this is a translation of the Greek word *metanoia*. *Metanoia* means 'beyond the mind' (just as 'metaphysical' means greater than the physical, super-natural). Here Jesus is using the expression at a deeper level than we use it in everyday conversation, meaning 'change your decision'. He means change your mind-set, change your attitudes, your paradigm, change your level of consciousness, which we might interpret as to transcend. This is born out by Jesus saying to the Jewish leader Nicodemus: 'No one can see the Kingdom of God unless he is born again' (John 3:3). The change of consciousness has to be as radical as that: to live in an entirely new dimension. Only in this way can we become Kingdom people.

The Kingdom can be neither experienced nor lived without this complete shift in consciousness. This implies a letting-go of everything we cling to for security. Two further parables illustrate this.

> The Kingdom of Heaven is like this. A man happens to find a treasure hidden in a field. He covers it up again, and is so happy that he goes and sells everything he has, and then goes back and buys that field.
>
> Also the Kingdom of Heaven is like this. A man is looking for fine pearls, and when he finds one that is unusually fine, he goes and sells everything he has, and buys that pearl. (Matthew 13: 44-45)

For the one authentic state of consciousness, Kingdom-consciousness, all lesser ways of knowing and perceiving have to be transcended.

That Kingdom-consciousness is not acquired by accumulating facts, by gathering information that comes to us from outside ourselves, through our senses, from other people. We call that rational knowledge because we receive it from without and then rationalise about it to make it our own. Kingdom-consciousness comes through intuitive knowledge. It comes to those who are receptive to an inner spark that gives us the wisdom to perceive, to experience, the presence of God active in all creation: that perception which increases our appreciation of our own worth and of others as divine.

In our science- and technology-driven world today humanity desperately needs a new vision to give meaning to life. A vision which elevates us above the rational, the material, the provable. Such a vision is not offered by repeating those expressions of Christian truths which were adequate in centuries past. Explanations of creation in a Garden of Eden, our descent from one pair of human beings, of evil resulting from The Fall, the traditional doctrine of Redemption by a blood sacrifice, are no longer compatible with the way we understand our life today, with what we know about our world, about Planet Earth's place in the Universe, about human psychology and about the workings of the mind. Explanations of our human condition and the means to better it that were offered by St Paul to his Greek and Jewish-influenced readership, adequate though they were for that time and culture, can no longer satisfy us. To continue to trot them out as the ultimate and eternal explanation simply discredits the power of the message of Jesus for today's spiritually starved population.

This is not to say that we throw overboard the accumulated wisdom of the past two millennia but that, building on that foundation, we attempt to re-express our beliefs in contemporary terms. We need to go back to that core message of Jesus — the Kingdom of God — and understand it as offering the vision that humanity craves today.

In this chapter I have painted the big picture of the Jesus vision. These ideas now need unpacking.

Some Interpretations of the Expression 'Kingdom of God'

* The world the way God means it to be.

* God's design that all humanity lives in harmony together and with the whole of creation.

* 'The new state of things, the new manner of being, of living, of living in community which the Gospel inaugurates'
  (Pope Paul VI — Evangelisation in the Modern World)

* 'A cosmic spiritual centre, a supreme pole of consciousness, upon which all the separate consciousnesses of the world may converge and within which they may love one another.'
  (Teilhard de Chardin — The Future of Man)

* The situation in which life is ordered by interior, spiritual power rather than by external human-controlled power.

* Living with the consciousness of God's all-pervading presence: that all creation is divine.

* The Kingdom of God ... means the divine life among men. This is the central message of all religion.
  (Bede Griffiths — Return to the Centre)

* A total, global and structural transfiguration and revolution of the reality of human beings; it is the cosmos purified of all evils and full of the reality of God. The Kingdom of God is not to be in another world but is the old world transformed into a new one.
  (Leonardo Boff — Jesus Christ Liberator)

6

THE MYSTERY
OF THE KINGDOM

Despite the fact that the Kingdom was the central point of Jesus' message, the proclamation of which was his life's purpose, he left us no clear, defined idea what he meant by 'The Kingdom of God'. It remains, and to us on Earth always will remain, a 'mystery'. When we speak of a religious concept or event as a mystery, we are not saying we cannot comprehend it. We are saying that because it contains an element of the absolute it has a dimension greater than we are able to grasp by reason. To define something is to confine it: to put it within parameters which enable us to contain it, to control it, to give it limits. We cannot box-in anything which has a divine element. To do so would be to confine God and to reduce Him to our mental limitations.

The Greek word for 'mystery' is *mysterion*, meaning a knowledge someone can acquire, not through an educational process, by inductive and deductive reasoning — the channel of exterior knowledge — but only through experience and insight: God revealing Truth through intuitive knowledge.

The Kingdom is not limited to a place nor to an event. Remembering that the gospels and letters of the New Testament were written in Greek, it is interesting to note that the Greek word used by their authors for 'Kingdom' is *basileia* which is literally translated as 'reign' and not 'realm' or 'domain'. The Kingdom is a symbol of the destiny God has designed for humanity — something we are always striving towards but which cannot be entirely grasped by our present limited consciousness. We need such symbols of the perfect future to compel us onwards just as the Israelites while wandering in the arid desert before entering their 'promised land' encouraged each other with a description of their future lying in a well-watered, fertile garden of plenty where all was harmony and where man and woman walked with God in bliss. This was for them the symbol of what God originally intended for humanity, and they called it Eden.

We attain a perception of the mystery of the Kingdom, not by hearing about it, but by experiencing it. And we experience it when we live according to its values, which is only possible after we have been through a conversion process which is so radical that it is like a rebirth. In the womb our eyes are closed, our world is minimal. At birth we have such a new experience that we enter a new level of consciousness: we see, we hear, we feel, we smell, we taste. We begin to 'know' our world; that is, to be aware of it, to interpret it, to interact with it. So great is the break-through to Kingdom awareness that Jesus uses this example of birth in his conversation with Nicodemus:

> I am telling you the truth: no one can see the Kingdom of God unless he is born again. No one can enter the Kingdom of God unless he is born of water and the Spirit (John 3:3,5).

Nicodemus was mystified by this as well he might have been. 'How can a grown man be born again?' he asks. In fact the Greek word translated as 'again' can also be rendered as 'from above'. To be born again is to attain a higher state of consciousness.

Some spiritual writers have interpreted Jesus' mention of water here to imply that such enlightenment comes only through Baptism and is in consequence the prerogative of Christians. This is not so. Water is symbolic of the fullness of life which comes from the power of the Spirit. Jesus goes on to say 'You must *all* be born again' (John 3:7), but not all in fact obtain this vision by receiving sacramental Baptism.

The majority of Jesus' Kingdom sayings are descriptive of the Kingdom rather than proclaiming it. And, being unable to define it, they come across with an air of mystery. For the ordinary people he had to use the symbolic language of the parable. To his disciples alone could he make the notion more explicit: 'The knowledge of the secrets of the Kingdom of God has been given to you, but to the rest it comes by means of parables' (Luke 8:10). Even so, right up to the last moment of their earthly contact with Jesus, at the moment of his Ascension, they asked him: 'Lord, will you at this time give the Kingdom back to Israel?' (Acts 1:6). It would take their enlightenment by the Spirit at Pentecost to enable them to reflect back on their years in the company of Jesus and perceive in it the full meaning of the Christ event.

'NOW' AND 'NOT YET'

Another aspect of the Kingdom which gives it an element of mystery, and one which continues to cause biblical scholars to write an endless number of explanatory papers, is the tension between the 'now' but 'not yet' of its fulfilment. Jewish writers before Jesus' time predicted that the Kingdom would come about as a great catastrophic, apocalyptic event, external to humanity. Jesus, on the other hand, sees the Kingdom coming about within his own person, by means of a powerful energy, already present and released through his own ministry. While John the Baptist's message was waiting for God to act, Jesus' message was that God is waiting for us to act. We could too easily excuse ourselves from any co-operation with Jesus' vision by saying it will be fulfilled only 'at the end of time'. True, it is God's Kingdom, He alone empowers it to become a reality but He chooses to involve us in bringing it about. Otherwise Jesus' instruction to his disciples to pray for its coming, 'Thy Kingdom come...', would be a charade. No, the end time happens when humanity has taken Jesus' formula for life sufficiently seriously that the Kingdom has become a reality, it has emerged through time. It will be the moment when there actually comes about on Earth that reality so beautifully described in the Catholic liturgy of the feast of Christ the King: 'An eternal and universal kingdom: a kingdom of truth and life, a kingdom of holiness and grace, a kingdom of justice, love and peace'. This double aspect of the Kingdom — as a reality of the present while being a reality of the future — is apparent in some of the parables in Matthew's gospel. It is apparent in the parables of chapter 13 (the sower, the weeds, the mustard seed, the yeast, the hidden treasure, the pearl, the net) as well as in others of his parables: the unforgiving servant (18:23-35), the workers in the vineyard (20:1- 16), the ten virgins (25:1-13).

Using the imagery of the parable of the treasure hidden in the field, we could tell it this way: God has already donated us a field, quite gratuitously, and He has made it known that the supreme treasure is buried there. So now we are in possession of that field but we are still trying to discover the treasure. We have not yet taken possession of the treasure, not yet claimed it.

This aspect of the mystery of the Kingdom becomes easier to understand when we regard its fulfilment as the eternal vision God has for humanity, indeed had since the beginning of time. In the eternal NOW of God, outside our creation-limitation of time, the Kingdom exists in its fullness because it is the fulfilment of God's vision which cannot be other than successful. In its working out, however, in the context of created time, it has its advances and its setbacks, it is incomplete, and is dependent upon our free co-operation with God for its actualisation in the space-time dimension. The second letter of Peter reminds us: 'There is no difference in the Lord's sight between one day and a thousand years' (3:8). (Hence the belief in the Middle Ages that each of the six days of creation represented a thousand years, so the Universe was six thousand years old!) He continues: 'The Lord is not being slow to carry out his promises...being patient with you all, wanting nobody to be lost and everybody to be brought to change his ways'; in other words, to *metanoia,* to a change of consciousness.

Within its being worked out in time there are moments when it takes a great leap forward.

The appearance of Jesus as the Christ two millennia ago contained the potential for the whole of humanity to take just such a great evolutionary leap towards our final destiny. One element of this potential is that Jesus made known to us that we have indeed a divine destiny. It is what Teilhard de Chardin called the Omega Point, the end point. The author of the Letter to the Church in Ephesus writes:

> God did what he had purposed, and made known to us the
> secret plan he had already decided to complete by means of
> the Christ. This plan which God will complete when the time

119

is right, is to bring all creation together, everything in the heavens and everything on Earth, with the Christ as head (1:9-10).

We find in this passage one of the phrases which is key to understanding the nature of the Kingdom: the unity of the whole of humanity in God.

We have to understand the words 'bring all creation together' and 'everything in the heavens' as expressions made within the limited knowledge of the author's time and not in the light of today's astrophysics. We have no reason to believe that Jesus' understanding of God's design applied beyond Planet Earth. The Jesus event, including his death and resurrection, has meaning and effect only for ourselves on this planet. Jesus' Kingdom proclamation has nothing to say about the Universe as a whole.

A COMPOSITE PICTURE

So Jesus was not able to give us any comprehensive formula to tell us exactly what he meant by the phrase 'the Kingdom of God'. He could only present us with the ingredients of a composite picture which, under the guidance of his Spirit, we have to put together ourselves. This collage is composed partly of parables, which of their nature are open-ended, non-defining, non-confining, having something to say to each of us according to our level of awareness. It is made up partly of Jesus' 'Magna Carta' of the Kingdom — the Sermon on the Mount (Matthew 5-7) — partly of his own way of life and the values he lived by: his sitting at table with sinners (Mark 2:15-17), his attitude towards lepers (Matthew 8:3), towards adulterers (John 8:3-11), towards tax-collectors (Luke 19:1-9) and towards other of society's outcasts (John 4:5-41). 'The person with Christ Consciousness sees all other human beings as the Christ and treats them accordingly' writes Jim Marion *(Putting on the Mind of Christ)*. His miracles too, which were themselves intended to be vehicles of the message, contribute to the overall picture. When John the Baptist's disciples were looking for a straight answer from Jesus to their question: 'Are you he who is to come, or should we expect someone else?' he referred them for an answer to his 'signs': 'Go back and tell John what you have seen and heard: the blind see again, the lame walk, lepers are cleansed, the deaf hear, the dead are raised to life and good news is preached to the poor' (Luke 7:22-23)

For those who were well disposed — 'those who had ears to hear and eyes to see' — the signs were there to be seen, signs that a new era had dawned. 'While Jesus was in Jerusalem during the Passover Festival many believed in him as they saw the miracles he performed' reports John (2:23).

But it was above all in his own person that the Kingdom was manifest, so that the gospel of Mark opens by declaring that the Good News is about Jesus: 'This is the Good News about Jesus the Christ, the Son of God'.

THREE EXPRESSIONS OF THE KINGDOM

Before proceeding further in our exploration of this Kingdom vision we need to clarify a confusion that arises between three expressions that we find in Scripture: Kingdom of God, Kingdom of Heaven and Kingdom of Christ. The expression 'Kingdom of Christ' and the implication that it is the Kingdom of Jesus rather than the Kingdom of God is not frequent. It is found only occasionally in the Gospels (Luke 22:30, 23:42; Matthew 13:41, 20:21; John 18:36) and would appear to be a notion that developed among the Apostles after Jesus' time. It is also mentioned five times in the Epistles and once in the Book of Revelation. The probable explanation for its appearance is that as the early Christians began to believe that Jesus was invested with the fulness of deity (Colossians 2:9) the term Christ and God became almost interchangeable. It is unlikely that Jesus himself ever spoke of the Kingdom as *his* Kingdom (with the exception of his remark to Pilate explaining that it was not a political entity) just as he never spoke of himself as God nor equal with God: 'I am going to the Father: he is greater than I' (John 14:28). Paul, as it were, decides the issue by explaining that at the end of time the Christ will hand over the Kingdom to God, although Jesus never called God a king:

> Then the end will come; the Christ will overcome all spiritual rulers, authorities and powers, and will hand over the Kingdom to God the Father ... When all things have been placed under the Christ's rule, then he himself, the Son, will place himself under God, who placed all things under him; and God will rule completely over all (I Corinthians 15:24-28).

Confusion can be caused for Catholics particularly by the celebration of the Feast of Christ the King on the last Sunday of the liturgical year. Few are aware that this feast was instituted in the mid-1920s to support the cause of the royal families of Europe when they were being threatened by the spread of socialism and democracy which was proclaimed by the Vatican as one of the evils of Modernism!

When Mark and Luke record Jesus as using the phrase 'Kingdom of God' Matthew records the same sayings with the expression 'Kingdom of Heaven'. In fact, of the forty-six times Matthew has Jesus speak of the Kingdom, only four times do we find the phrase 'Kingdom of God'. Since Matthew's gospel was writen for Jewish Christians, it respects their custom of using a circumlocution in place of the holy name of God, just as we might exclaim 'Heaven help us' when we are really calling for God's help, or 'Heaven knows' rather than 'God knows'. Unfortunately, preachers in our own time do their congregations a disservice by using the term 'Kingdom of Heaven' as frequently as 'Kingdom of God' and thereby unwittingly cause the vision of our future to be presented as a beyond-death reality.

Although in John's gospel the expression 'Kingdom' is used only twice — both times in Jesus' dialogue with Nicodemus (3:3,5) — it is the most constantly recurring subject in the other three gospels, being mentioned a hundred and four times, ninety-one times on the lips of Jesus: by Matthew forty-six times, by Luke thirty-one times and by Mark fourteen times. It is the subject of almost all the parables, of which forty tell us what the Kingdom is like and twenty-five warn about the fate of those who are unprepared for the Kingdom.

TEACHING AND PREACHING

Jesus communicated his oral message in two forms. A verse in Matthew's gospel distinguishes between his teaching and his preaching: 'Jesus went all over Galilee, teaching in the synagogues, preaching Good News about the Kingdom' (4:23). His preaching is the announcement that the new and last age of the Kingdom has arrived: his teaching is about the demand that this event makes of us, the nature of the conversion that acceptance of this Good News will bring about. The preaching and the teaching are complementary aspects of his message.

Fortunately for us the Good News of the Kingdom is not confined to the realm of thoughts and beliefs. It was not an academic teaching offered to a Scribal school trained in the Law of Moses. If it were, our holiness would depend upon our erudition, our theological comprehension. It is about being raised to a new level of awareness which injects new life into our attitudes and actions because we recognise and own our divinity. It is an awarenes of our potential and of our relationship to God, of our ability to live right now as sharers in the life of God. It is an insight available to professor and peasant alike.

While it is a remarkable characteristic of Jesus' preaching and teaching that he was willing to share his message with anyone who would listen, we notice, nevertheless, that he was careful to offer people no more of his teaching than they were ready to hear and able to accept. To the general public he gave basic ethical norms to enable them to live more in accordance with God's design for humanity. By his employing parables (Matthew 13:34) each listener was able to comprehend his teaching at their own level of consciousness.

However, to a chosen few — his disciples — it would seem that he imparted a higher teaching. 'The knowledge of the secrets of the Kingdom of God has been given to you,' he told them, 'but to the rest it comes by means of parables' (Luke 8:10). Mark writes: 'He spoke the word to them [the crowd] as far as they were capable of understanding it ... but he explained everything to his disciples when they were alone' (4:33-34). Among the Apostles, Peter, James and John were given more advanced teaching and allowed a mystical experience on Mount Tabor: the event we call the Transfiguration (Matthew 17:1-9). Jesus even said he would not 'give to dogs what is holy or throw [his] pearls before swine' (Matthew 7:6). We can only conjecture that, in line with the other Great Masters, his 'pearls' were a ritual or a technique for entering into a deeper level of consciousness in which the divine indwelling could be experienced.

Why, we reasonably ask, was this initiation not handed down by the Apostles? Why was it lost to us? Since the Gospel writers and St Paul wrote for the general public, their writings do not include the private instructions the disciples received. As the young Church grew it created a single code of doctrine that was meant for the masses. Thus the Church's ethics, ritual and dogma have become identified as the teaching of Jesus and so we can be forgiven for thinking that he never taught the higher spiritual path.

Apart from Jerusalem he appears not to have taught in any of the major towns of Judea or Galilee, but confined himself to obscure villages, to places such as Nazareth and Capernaum, which were obscure enough not even to obtain a mention in the Hebrew Scriptures. Indeed, he himself gave as a sign of his credentials to the inquiring disciples of John the Baptist that 'good news is preached to the poor' (Matthew 11:5) as a fulfilment of the prophecy of Isaiah about the Messiah (Isaiah 61:1).

Since the proclamation of the Kingdom was 'what God sent him to do', not only do we see it as the focal point of his preaching, but all the events and activities of his life centre upon this mission. His healing miracles were a sign of the Kingdom being already present: a sign of the fulfilment of prophecy and as a conquering of the opposite forces, the forces of evil (Luke 11:20). His cosmic miracles, upon the elements and material things, were the consequence of the power possessed by a fully enlightened human being. His feasting and banquets were messianic signs that God's new era had come as well as being occasions for breaking down the social and cultural barriers between the 'clean' and 'unclean'. His re-casting of the Jewish laws — 'You have heard how it was said ... but I tell you ...' (Matthew chapter 5) — are a sign of the liberated Kingdom person living at a deeper level of consciousness with greater sensitivity and awareness. He was 'excommunicated', thrown out of the Temple and received the death penalty because he challenged the way religion was being presented. His very torture and cruel death were a direct consequence of the non-acceptability of his message by those who felt their authority and position to be threatened by him. His resurrection, his attaining a new quality of life through the passage of death, was a natural outcome for a totally fulfilled person (Romans 1:4), the one in whom the vision of God had become a reality.

JESUS, A NEW-ERA PERSON

This is not the place to present yet another life of Jesus, but since both his style of life and the values by which he lived illustrate what he was preaching as well as being the cause of its coming about, it is necessary to highlight certain aspects of his life so that our reading of the gospels can be from this Kingdom perspective. Jesus not only proposes an ideal but in his person bridges the gap between the ideal and reality.

The Decree of the Second Vatican Council of the Catholic Bishops (1962-1965) on the nature of the Church states that: 'In Christ's *word*, in his *works* and in his *presence* this Kingdom reveals itself to us... The *miracles* of Jesus also confirm that the Kingdom has already arrived on Earth... Before all things, however, the Kingdom is clearly visible in *the very person* of Christ' (LG.5. Italics added).

Jesus expressed his own experience as living as a new-era person in his saying 'I and the Father are one' and he prayed for his closest friends 'that they may be one just as you and I are one' (John 17:11). This knowing of oneself as divine is the act of being born into the Kingdom. 'This conscious life in God is one of unimaginable wealth and abundance and energy and unwavering humble recognition of the sacredness of all things and beings, of the Kingdom "inside" and "outside"', writes Andrew Harvey in *Son of Man*.

We have always to keep in mind when reading the gospels that the evangelists were not taking down a dictation of Jesus' words at the time he spoke them, but writing many years afterwards, with the hindsight given them by the inspiration of the Spirit at Pentecost, and writing for particular groups of Christians with different backgrounds. The probable reason why the main thrust of the apostles' preaching was about the person of Jesus as the epitome of Good News, rather than about the Kingdom, — the expression 'Kingdom of God' appears only seven times in the Acts of the Apostles, mostly in reporting Paul's preaching — was that while the expression had great historical significance for the Jews, it would have meant little to Greek-culture Christians. Therefore the Apostles did not hesitate to identify the person of Jesus with the Good News and the Kingdom. For instance, where Luke quotes Jesus as saying: 'I assure you that anyone who leaves home or wife or brothers or parents or children for the sake of the Kingdom of God will receive much more in this present age...' (Luke 18:29), Mark, writing for Gentile converts, quotes: 'I tell you that anyone who leaves home or brothers or sisters or mother or father or children or fields for me and for the gospel...' (Mark 10:29).

In John's gospel, written very much later than the other three — perhaps as much as seventy years after the

Resurrection — and from a quite different perspective, the identification of Jesus with the Kingdom is even more explicit. In fact, as mentioned above, the word 'Kingdom' only occurs twice in this gospel, apart from Jesus referring to 'my kingdom' in his few words with Pilate, on which occasion he describes his mission by saying: 'I was born and came into the world for this one purpose, to speak about the truth' (John 18:36,37). The implication is that it is only through accepting the truth of his announcement of the Kingdom, only through faith in him as the one who makes the Kingdom a reality, that the Kingdom can become a reality in our own lives.

While the other three evangelists have Jesus declare his message in terms of the Kingdom, John has him declare it in terms of 'life', the fullness of life. That for John is what the Kingdom is all about. God's vision, as Jesus understood it, is that we should all attain fullness of life, the fullness of our humanity, in union with God. The word 'life' or 'eternal life' occurs in John's gospel thirty-six times, and it recounts Jesus as expressing his mission in the words: 'I have come in order that you might have life - life in all its fullness' (John 10:10). Jesus understood himself to be a channel of God's life to us, and our means to receive this divine life already now in its fullness is to live our lives in the Jesus way. 'Anyone who believes in the Son has eternal life, but anyone who refuses to believe in the Son will never see life' (John 3:36). Thus it is not only Jesus and the Kingdom that John identifies but both in turn are related to divine life.

While Jesus himself proclaims the Kingdom, the early Church of the Apostles proclaimed Jesus. And yet it is abundantly clear from the accounts that the gospels give us that Jesus did not ask his disciples to rally round his person as an object of cult or respect. Indeed, unlike

128

the prophets before him, and unlike gurus in other religions, whose followers were those who gathered round them voluntarily rather than by call, Jesus deliberately chose 'the Twelve'. With his vision of the Kingdom as a new era in human history that was destined to grow ever outwards from its tiny beginning (the mustard seed), he needed a group to share his mission with him. The choice of the men he made, therefore, is instructive. Since he was not founding a new religion nor a new institution, he did not require men who could assimilate and then proclaim convincingly a new doctrine, nor men possessing organisational ability. He required men who were open enough to be touched by the radical nature of his message, men who would be fired with enthusiasm because they had experienced in his company a new and exciting way of living, a new attitude to religious values, a new appreciation of the worth of each human person, and above all, a new intimate way of relating to God.

A NEW WAY OF RELATING TO GOD

This last point, of Jesus introducing us to a quite new relationship with God, needs special emphasis because it is the key to understanding what was so new in Jesus' message and why its acceptance causes us to make a quantum leap towards our final goal, which we call the fullness of the Kingdom.

While it is true that we find God referred to as the father of the nation in the writings of the Hebrew Testament, the title is used to indicate God's care for his people as their creator, the supplier of their needs, the winner of their battles. Jesus uses the title 'Father' to speak of God with an entirely different meaning and value, with affection. It was a shift from a father-of-the-tribe experience to a father-of-each-individual-person experience.

> It seems likely that during the two or three years of his public ministry Jesus was one of several Galilean preachers and healers who stressed God's fatherly love and were critical of the more legalistic religion of the priesthood at the Jerusalem Temple. He was intensely conscious of God's holy and loving presence, a presence that was as real to him as the hills and lake of Galilee. To live in this consciousness is already to be in God's Kingdom and he sought to bring others to share that consciousness and to live the life of the Kingdom in the here and now (John Hick *The Fifth Dimension*).

Jesus understood himself to be chosen to live in this quite intimate, personal relationship to God: 'The Father chose me and sent me into the world' (John 10:36). His mission was centred on the absolute power of God operating through him. All the good he did he attributed to God (John 5:19,30), while he was extremely reserved in speaking about himself (Luke 10:22). He took great pains not to be deified or adored. After some of his miracles he instructed those healed to go to the Temple to offer thanks to God, even though he had so passionately identified God's cause with his own that he was able to heal (Luke 9:42-43) and to forgive sin in his own name (Luke 5:20-21). He never claimed to be omnipotent (Mark 6:5), nor omniscient (Matthew 24:36), nor even completely good (Luke 18:19). Nor did he claim what the Council of Nicaea claimed for him three centuries later: that he was God the Son. We only know of one occasion when Jesus introduced himself and that was to St Paul on the road to Damascus. Even though this occurred after his Resurrection, he did not entitle himself 'The Christ' but 'I am Jesus of Nazareth' (Acts 22:8). He claimed by his miracles that his power flowed from his having attained consciousness of his divine identity as a human being. We would say today that he had attained 'enlightenment'.

Nowhere is his relationship with God more clear than in the way he addresses God and speaks of God as his father in that intimate family term 'Abba', an Aramaic word which is probably the most historically authentic word we have of Jesus. He is recorded as using the expression '*my* father' forty-six times. Indeed, such is his obsession with God as father that there are few pages of the gospels that do not carry some such reference.

Since this intimacy with God was in stark contrast with the traditional way of relating to God, it seems to have been noted by the evangelists as expressing the root of his spirituality. 'I am in the Father and the Father is in me' (John 14:11), 'The Father and I are one' (John 10:30). It led to his fellow villagers from Nazareth being scandalised by him: who does he think he is, this carpenter, this son of Mary whose brothers are James, Joseph, Judas and Simon? They rejected him (Mark 6:1-3). It would eventually lead him to the cross on a charge of blasphemy: 'You are only a man, but you are trying to make yourself God' (John 10:33), which of course he was not trying to do.

This new relationship between God and humanity understood and lived by Jesus is, with all its consequences the very essence of Kingdom living, because one of those consequences is that, accepting a common father, we are required to accept, love and treat every other human being as our sister and brother whatever our differences in culture, national loyalty or religious persuasion. This provides the formula for a new world order indeed. It is the only explanation for the openness of Jesus to all people without exception, cutting through all the barriers

131

the Law and custom had set up. Even the Pharisees who were trying to entrap him had to admit: 'Teacher, we know that you tell the truth. You teach the truth about God's will for humanity without worrying about what people think, because you pay no attention to a person's status' (Matthew 22:16).

St Paul glimpsed the wonder of this vision: '... there is no longer any distinction between Gentiles and Jews, circumcised and uncircumcised, barbarians, savages, slaves and free persons, but the Christ is all, the Christ is in all' (Colossians 3:11). It is, however, so new, so radical, so unbelievably utopian, that even after two thousand years since this breakthrough there are few signs that the invitation is being taken seriously. Even those of us who are his declared followers today have great difficulty in turning from a Hebrew Testament God 'out there' to feel comfortable with a God with whom we can relate intimately, with affection and address as 'friend'.

A BATTLE AGAINST EVIL

In carrying his hearers towards the fullness of life, Jesus saw himself battling with all forms of negativity. In the language of his time and his religious culture he expressed this as a battle between two kingdoms: the reign or power of God overcoming the reign of Satan. The stage was set when he first took on his role, in the scene described as the Temptations in the Desert. He saw all aspects of his mission as a fight against evil. When the seventy-two disciples returned from their mission they reported: 'Lord, even the demons obeyed us when we gave them a command in your name' and he replied: 'I saw Satan fall like lightening from heaven' (Luke 10:17-18). The Church speaks of Jesus as a Saviour. His saving task was to be a liberator from all that is negative, oppressive, alienating, impoverishing. His is a power that makes whole, that makes us fully human, that gives 'life in abundance'. Perhaps no account of Jesus' healing ministry better demonstrates his power to make whole and better describes, in a language loaded with symbolism, the divisive power of evil, than that of his casting the 'unclean spirit' out of the man in the territory of the Gerasenes, (Mark 5:1-20). The man is described as living 'among the tombs'. He is not only ritually unclean but associated with death and decay. He is quite uncontrollable and of astonishing strength. No number of chains and irons could hold him: the strength of evil power is not to be underestimated. His 'wandering through the hills, screaming and cutting himself with stones' tells of his disorientation, and the self-destructive nature of evil. He is no longer an integrated person — 'My name is Legion' — but disintegrated enough to take possession of two thousand pigs! Jesus' healing energy restored him to wholeness, holiness and self-respect. We are told 'he was sitting there clothed and in his right mind'.

Jesus' forgiveness of sins is another aspect of his liberating action, and in a cultural context which was particularly prone to see any kind of suffering to be the consequence of sin (John 9:2), he dedicated himself especially to seek out those who were designated or thought of themselves as sinners: 'I have not come to call respectable people but outcasts' (Mark 2:18). The Judaism of Jesus' time, unlike classical Judaism, was particularly preoccupied with the influence of demons — which may be why the Christian tradition has been over-concerned with Satan and his devils for so many centuries — such that the suffering of the blind, the deaf, the dumb, the epileptic was attributed to evil spirits. Jesus' miracles

133

of physical healing, therefore, were never meant to be a presentation of his credentials as a man of God, not done to win acclaim, — in fact he often insists that news of his miracles is not to be spread (Mark 5:43) — but victorious events of God's Kingdom over that of the Evil One. His curing leprosy and paralysis was a liberating of people from a form of bondage to make them whole. It was a proclamation of his message in action.

His acts of breaking down the cultural and social barriers, seen particularly in his eating habits, were also done to heal the divisions between different groups of people. On one occasion he will eat with sinners and publicans (Luke 15:2). On another, he will accept the table hospitality of the Pharisees (Luke 7:36-50). This is particularly significant when we remember that in the Jewish prophecies the banquet was a metaphor for describing the Kingdom. It was on the occasion of banquets that Jesus delivered some of his most beautiful parables.

Jesus' various actions to overthrow the demonic power structure should not obscure from our view just how creative and up-building and positive his mission and his message were. He was concerned to 'make all things new' and so many of his parables are about growth (see all those in Matthew chapter 13 and Mark chapter 4).

A UNIVERSAL MESSAGE

One aspect of the positive, creative character of Jesus' mission is the universality of his message. It is not a judgement of vengeance on sinners and the godless, in the line of the Hebrew prophets, as expressed for example by the Qumran community and John the Baptist, but a healing, energising message of peace and joy. It is significant that when Jesus declared his manifesto in the

Nazareth synagogue (Luke 4:16-19), when he first went public, he did so by quoting Isaiah (61:1-2) which describes the coming of God's Kingdom. Jesus concludes the quotation: 'The time has come when the Lord will save his people' but omits to add the following line from Isaiah: 'and defeat their enemies'. There is to be no longer a division between a Chosen People and their enemies. What is going to be decisive for people is not membership of Israel but a personal conversion: a change from a self-centred life to a life given to and for others.

Jesus made the dream of a new era a reality precisely by living as a new era person. By living and by relating to people with the belief that the new era had already come, not with a 'let's pretend' approach but with the conviction that with and through him it actually had become visible, and by his very living of these new era values, he *did* make it a reality and this was why he was recognised as having a different kind of authority from the Scribes (Matthew 7:29) — and the Scribes at the time had considerable authority. They were one of the three dominant classes of Jewish society, rivalling the priestly aristocracy (the Chief Priests) and the lay nobility (the Elders). Their authority derived not from their birth nor from their wealth but from their learning. The authority of Jesus was of quite a different kind. It lay in the authenticity of his message (Luke 4:22), which was recognisable to all of good will. While the Scribes' authority was a legal, institutionalised authority, that of Jesus derived from his own personal charism. He frequently appeals for faith from his listeners, but it is not for faith in God nor for faith in his own divinity but for faith in himself as a trailblazer, as the one who ushers in the new era. He did not see himself as unique, nor even as possessing divine powers which were unique, otherwise he would not have said: 'Whoever believes in me will do what I do — yes, he will do even greater things' (John 14:12). The faith he asks for is an invitation, a plea to share in his own belief that the new era comes about by being lived. The same plea is made to all people today as it has been through every age. The new era will become a reality, the end time will be reached, when we can take the great leap forward into an entirely new manner of living, regulating our lives by the values he gave us.

'This resounding motif of Jesus' message — the imminent Kingdom of God — must be recovered as a key to the whole of Christian theology' (Wolfhard Pannenberg *Theology and the Kingdom of God*).

WHAT CAN WE KNOW ABOUT JESUS ?

A FAMILIAR TRADITIONAL UNDERSTANDING

AN EMERGING CONTEMPORARY UNDERSTANDING

Jesus' actions and words are accurately recorded in the gospels.

Jesus is the person of whom the gospels speak: a product of memory, reflection, revision and community experience.

Starting from our knowledge of God we discover who Jesus is as the Christ. We know the qualities of Jesus because we know the attributes of God.

Starting from what we know of the historical man, Jesus, we learn from him what we can of the mystery of God. We know some of the attributes of God because we see the sort of person Jesus was.

God 'sent' his Scn 'down' to earth, and Jesus ascended 'up' into Heaven.

We do not think of the Incarnation or the Ascension as physically down or up. We understand them as metaphors.

Jesus is God-made-man who came down from Heaven to save us.

Jesus is a manifestation of God who lived among us to show and empower us to live by higher values — which he called 'The Kingdom of God'. This perception was a radical step forward in humanity's understanding of its call to At-one-ment with the Divine nature.

The accounts of Jesus' birth given in the Bible, in partiticular that "he came down from Heaven by the power of the Holy Spirit and became incarnate from the Virgin Mary", are literally true.

Jesus was conceived naturally and born as a human baby to a young woman (the original translation of 'virgin'). The accounts of his birth were constructed later to explain his divine nature in mythological terms.

The emphasis is on the Divinity of Jesus.

Today's emphasis is on the humanity of Jesus and his God-consciousness.

Jesus is God, a Divine Being who took on a human nature.

Jesus, in his humanity, is one who is transparent to the Divine. God was as fully present and active in Jesus as is possible in human form.

Jesus is worthy of unconditional worship as God.

We worship God as revealed in Jesus and we pray to God through Jesus.

Jesus was omniscient and omnipotent from his conception.

Jesus was limited by his humanity. His understanding of himself, of his mission and of God developed during his lifetime.

A FAMILIAR TRADITIONAL UNDERSTANDING	AN EMERGING CONTEMPORARY UNDERSTANDING
Everything Jesus did and said is done and said by God. He had supernatural powers because he was God.	Jesus acted and spoke as a human being. All his powers issued from his potential being fully realised: because he was fully aware of and lived his unity with God.
His miracles prove he was God.	His miracles are signs of the presence of God's Kingdom.
From Jesus' words: 'I am the way, the truth and the life; no one goes to the Father except by me', we understand that Christianity alone possessses the true revelation. All other religions are false or inadequate.	The way to God is also found in other religions which have different perspectives on the one Truth. But for Christians its manifestation in Jesus is the most accessible, powerful and inspiring.
Jesus was sent down to Earth by his Father to shed his blood for our 'Salvation': variously described as Ransom, a price paid, Justification, Satisfaction, Reparation.	Jesus was murdered on account of his faithfulness in carrying out his mission. He brought about the possibility of At-one-ment: a step forward in humanity's evolution towards our becoming one with the Divine.
Redemption is an act of rescue by an external, Divine agent.	Redemption is the transformation process by which the life-giving Spirit within us moves us from human-centredness to Divine-centredness.
Jesus is the Saviour of the world.	There is no indication in what are thought to be the authentic words of Jesus that he thought of himself as the Saviour of the world, nor that he understood his death to have a salvific value.
The 'Resurrection' is the belief that God raised Jesus to bodily life on the third day after he died on the cross.	The 'Resurrection' is the way in which St Paul and the evangelists affirm that Jesus is among us in a new manner of living, in a finer spiritual manner, thus demonstrating the power of divine love over material limitations.
Jesus is the full and the final revelation of God, which is to be guarded against corruption.	There is a continuing development in our understanding of the meaning of the Jesus event.

7

THE DIMENSIONS
OF THE KINGDOM

On account of the identification of the Kingdom with the Church for most of two millennia a question often arises about membership of the Kingdom. Is it an 'organisation', a 'body', which some people join and others do not, either by free choice or for sheer ignorance that there be a Kingdom? The very question reveals an institutional notion of the Kingdom. The Kingdom is not an institution but God's vision for the whole of humanity living with the consciousness of God's all-pervading presence, an awareness that all creation is divine, which awareness will dictate our manner of living and relating. Kingdom living means, in the words of George Fox, founder of the Quakers, recognising 'that of God in everyman'. Or today we would be more likely to add 'and in everything'. This is not a new idea. We find this ability to recognise the divine spark in all life affirmed by Plotinus and by many mystics, Dionysius, Eckhart, Ruysbroeck, Suso, Tauler among others. In the East it is the meaning of the universal buddha nature. In the words of Swami Dayatmananda of the Ramakrishna Mission: 'Hindus believe that each soul is potentially divine and the goal is to manifest this divinity. All of life is a school which helps each one of us to manifest his or her potential divinity'. And it is strongly affirmed by the Sufi mystics of Islam.

A common theme of mystics of all traditions is that our journey towards *atman*, our own divinisation, is by transcending our natural self-centredness. The Eastern Orthodox understanding of 'salvation' is our transformation into the finite 'likeness' of God. Julian of Norwich rejected the Fall-Redemption model of salvation, which demands a 'transaction' between human beings and God in the person of Jesus, which concentrates our minds on sin and guilt, and said that rather than guilt, which separated us from God, it was the spiritual confusion and blindness of our earthly state, our ego. This is not far removed from the notion of eastern religions that our greatest handicap to enlightenment is our ignorance.

We Christians regard Jesus as the most God-filled human being we know. He was intensely conscious of God's loving presence, of the divine in all people and all nature. Living in this consciousness meant that he was already living in the Kingdom and he sought to bring others to share that consciousness. The prayer he taught us to say — what we call the Lord's Prayer — includes the wish that 'thy will be done' (according to Matthew's version) following on immediately from 'thy Kingdom come'. In other words, a plea that God's vision be actualised already now in our midst: 'on earth as it is in heaven'.

We notice that Jesus never described anyone as being in the Kingdom, which would have had the implication that some were outside the Kingdom, although twenty five of his sixty five Kingdom parables are about the fate of those who are unprepared for the Kingdom, or should we say who are unco-operative in bringing it about, or even militating against its realisation. He did, however, tell the lawyer who quizzed him about the greatest commandment: 'You are not far from the Kingdom of God' (Mark 12:34). The lawyer was nearer the point of experiencing the Kingdom because he had the right understanding about the priority of loving God and neighbour over the offering of animals and sacrifices to God. He was heading in the right direction.

Years later, St Paul was to become very impatient with the petty squabbles among the Christians in Rome as to which kind of food was ritually clean and which unclean. He had to remind them that 'God's Kingdom is not a matter of eating and drinking, but of the righteousness, peace and joy which the Holy Spirit gives' (Romans 14:17). 'Righteousness' is a word that sounds somewhat pompous to our ears today. It was current in the Hebrew world to refer to keeping ritual observances, which is why, perhaps, we very rarely find it used by Jesus. Matthew is the only one who puts this word on Jesus' lips. In the context in which Paul uses the word here it is better understood as 'right relationships', the fruits of which are peace and joy. The righteousness of Jesus is love for others. In I Corinthians 6:9 Paul announces that the unrighteous will not possess God's Kingdom, and he goes on to give a list of those he considers to be the unrighteous: 'people of immoral lives, idolaters, adulterers, catamites, sodomites, thieves, usurers, drunkards, slanderers and swindlers — none of these will possess God's Kingdom'. He saw these people as having one thing in common: disfunctional relationships. The Kingdom, understood as the fulfilment of relationships, gives us a different way of appreciating so many of our Christian beliefs. (See diagram page 142)

There are two points Paul is making in his admonition to the Romans. The first is that the Kingdom is not

141

The Kingdom, understood as the fulfilment of relationships, gives coherence to our Christian beliefs.

KINGDOM: understood as right relating. (Rom. 14:17)

HEAVEN: when relationships are experienced to perfection.

CO-CREATORS: building the right environment for our relationships to grow.

EUCHARIST: the celebration of our community relationships in Christ.

SIN: the destruction of relationships

PRAYER: the language of community relationships.

HELL: when there is an irreparable absence of relationships.

RECONCILIATION: the healing of relationships.

VIRTUE: all the good acts which build up relationships.

THE CHURCH: the sign and promoter of the ideal ways of relating.

BAPTISM: our commitment to develop relationships in Christ.

furthered by the observance of laws and regulations (the old form of righteousness) but by our right relationships, which calls for an entirely new mode of living.

The second point he makes is that this new way of living is the fruit of the Holy Spirit. As God's will for us, it is God's gift; not something we can bring about by our own effort. As a dream for our future it is as utopian as the Marxist dream, and is just as concerned with our relationship to this Earth's goods, but differs essentially in the way it is to come about. It is not a human product but brought about by divine energy.

Jesus' parable about the growth of the seed has a lot to tell us of God's part and our part in the processes of making the Kingdom a reality:

> 'A man scatters seed in his field. He sleeps at night, is up and about during the day, and all the while the seeds are sprouting and growing. Yet he does not know how it happens. The soil itself makes the plants grow and bear fruit; first the tender stalk appears, then the ear, and finally the ear full of corn. When the corn is ripe, the man starts cutting it with his sickle, because harvest time has come' (Mark 4:26-29).

The seed once planted grows with an inevitability and according to a pattern predetermined by the species of seed. It is God who gives the growth, not us. Nevertheless, to bring the process to its finale our co-operation is asked for, to sow the seed in the first instance (and no doubt to fertilise and weed during the growth) then to harvest at the right moment. But our part in the growth of the Kingdom is no more than co-operative. Our co-operation hastens its fulfilment. So Peter writes: 'Do your best to make it come soon' (II Peter 3:12).

This is why Jesus never told us to build the Kingdom, but he did invite us to 'enter' it (Mark 10:15, 23-25). Perhaps this is better translated as to enter into:

143

to enter into its spirit, to enter its dimension, to be possessed by it, to be born again. The author of the Letter to the Ephesians explains: 'Your hearts and minds must be made completely new, and you must put on the new self, which is created in God's likeness and reveals itself in the true life that is upright and holy' (4:23-24). Only by entering into the spirit of it does it take hold of us. Only by getting into the water and starting to swim do we get the feel of swimming and so learn to swim. No amount of telling us about it turns us into swimmers. By living it we become 'actualisers' of the Kingdom. Like the seed, it grows outwards from within.

Are there, then, those who do not enter into the Kingdom way of life? Are they excluded from the Kingdom? What of the millions who have never had the chance to hear the Good News of Jesus the Christ?

When we consider the Kingdom in its plenitude as the accomplishment of God's vision for the fulfilment of each person within the unity of humanity, then it is clear that everyone born into this world is potentially a 'member', a part, of God's Kingdom whether conscious of their destiny or not. God's designs would be frustrated if every single person were not offered, in mysterious ways known only to God, the opportunity of full participation in the Kingdom, of 'reaching to the very height of Christ's full stature' (Ephesians 4:13), of living with Christ consciousness.

PARTICIPATION IN THE KINGDOM

The phrase 'participation in the Kingdom' can mean two things. It can mean living with a consciousness of our wonderful destiny and of what Jesus has revealed to us about it, and so living our lives as a response to this

144

invitation, as Kingdom people. By living by the values of the Kingdom one is actively, and even purposefully, making the Kingdom a reality in this present time. But they also participate in the furthering of God's vision, even quite unconsciously, who by any deed contribute to the uniting of people and to personal growth towards full humanity. Let me give two examples of this.

While I was living in Zambia, thousands of labourers from mainland China — Mau's atheists all of them - worked for several years to build a railway from the coast of Tanzania into Zambia. They would have been uncomprehending if they had been told that they were furthering the Kingdom of God in that part of the world. Nothing would have been more remote from their intention. But in fact, by opening up great areas of both countries by this new form of communication, that is just what they were doing: they were improving the quality of life of thousands of peasant farmers, enabling them to live lives that were more fully human and therefore more in conformity with God's dream for them.

I believe the greatest Kingdom-promoting events the world has yet known, happened in recent times. They were inspired, not by the United Nations, nor by any joint action of the Churches or world religions. They were the inspiration of a member of a pop music group, the Boomtown Rats. Urged by the need to raise money for the starving millions of Africa, Bob Geldof organised first a mammoth concert — Live Aid — concurrently in London and Philadelphia, lasting sixteen hours and watched by an estimated one thousand five hundred million people in one hundred and sixty countries, breaking all television audience records. That was on July 13th, 1985. This was followed on May 25th 1986 by an even more all-encompassing event: Sport Aid. Watched by the same mass TV audience, thirty million people in two hundred and seventy two cities across seventy eight countries ran a sponsored 10km, not to mention participation in every other conceivable form of sport, in an act of solidarity with the poorest in Africa. More recently, in October 1999, NetAid, (so-called because the event could be seen in its entirety on the Internet) the biggest charity music event since Live Aid, reached global viewing figures of one billion, a sixth of the world's population, with overlapping concerts held in London, New York and Geneva, featuring some of music's biggest names. The message of the concerts was that the developed world should band together to alleviate the burden of debt on developing nations. The proceeds from the London concert at the Wembley stadium went to refugees in Kosovo and Sudan.

Why do I call these Kingdom-promoting events? Never before, in the whole of human history, have so many people been united across all barriers of language, culture, ideologies and religions, in so many countries, in one common action: to raise money for the less fortunate. In terms of the description of God's vision in Ephesians 1:10 — the unification of all creation — these were indeed great religious acts. 'What God the Father considers to be pure and genuine religion is this: to take care of orphans and widows in their suffering...'(James 1:27).

THE 'PROFESSIONALS'

These were one-off events. But there is in the world a minority group of professionals. I call them 'professionals' because they profess to have pledged themselves to a lifelong commitment to live by and to be a witness to the values Jesus preached, for the sake of furthering the Kingdom vision. This group, calling itself the Church, has been described by the participating bishops of the Second Vatican Council in these words:

> 'The Church... receives the mission to proclaim and establish among all peoples the Kingdom ... of God. It becomes on Earth the initial budding forth of that Kingdom... the Church strains towards the consummation of the Kingdom...'(LG.5)

The Church understands itself as being entrusted with the task of continuing in each age the proclamation of the Good News of Jesus; of making known the wonderful things that God is doing in His world, as Jesus explained them to us. The role of the Church is to be the Sacrament of the Kingdom: the outward sign (by its values and community relationships) of the Spirit's inner workings to bring about God's design. To say that where the Church is not present the Good News is not available (Romans 10:14-15) is not at all the same thing as saying that those who are not Christians are not also, in some mysterious way, empowered to make their contribution to the coming of the Kingdom, as we have seen above with the Chinese railway builders.

Various attempts have been made to explain how this can be. The German theologian Karl Rahner, for instance, coined the expression 'anonymous Christians' to describe those who under, but unaware of, the Christ's influence are agents of the Kingdom. It is an unfortunate expression, not only because it is offensive to members of other religions — we would not like the Hindus to call us anonymous Hindus — but because to be a Christian means to be a disciple of Jesus the Christ and one cannot be a follower of Jesus without expressing that commitment. Any person may act 'christianly', that is according to the values of the Christ, but that is quite different from making a specific commitment to continue

Jesus' mission to the world, which commitment is made through the sacrament of Baptism in which one acknowledges Jesus the Christ as Lord of one's life and vows to convert oneself to live by his standards. Perhaps such persons would be better described as 'non-conscious Kingdom participants', their participation varying with their degree of being, even unknowingly, contributors to the making-present of the Kingdom.

There are moments in the life of even the apparently most wicked people when we notice some expression of altruistic love, some kindly deed. Despite the fact that study of the behaviour of the primates reveals that the roots of 'good behaviour' lie in the survival instinct, so that we can say that altruism appears to be explainable as the most advantageous move in the survival game (if we are nice to others we can assume they will be nice to us) this does not detract from the fact that any good deeds are furthering the coming of the Kingdom whether done consciously for that reason or not.

An African theologian, Laurenti Magesa, prefers the expression 'The New People of God'. Just as in the Hebrew Testament the 'People of God' were the people of just one small race (the Israelites) who considered themselves to be chosen by God to prepare humanity for the moment when the Messiah would come, so the New People of God of our own post-Jesus era, are made up of all people, world-wide, who co-operate with God's vision, the Kingdom. They are the unifiers of humanity who form a fellowship through their common intention, albeit an invisible fellowship. They are inspired by an inner conviction that the world has a better future which is not necessarily expressed in Christian terms.

Some of these New People of God commit themselves to witness to God's Kingdom within the visible community called Church. On the other hand, not all who would call themselves Church members can be included among the New People of God, because for some their Church membership is no more than a sociological fact which came about by their baptism as infants, but they have never been required to make an explicit profession of their commitment. Their membership of the Church has not been the means of their acquiring an inner conviction of their calling to promote the unity of all peoples.

THE SOCIAL AND PERSONAL DIMENSIONS

There are two further dimensions of the Kingdom revealed by Jesus which complement each other. The Kingdom has a social dimension: it is about the way people relate to each other — and this after all is what we shall be judged upon (Matthew 25:31-46) — and it is all about the unity of the whole of humanity with the Christ as head (Ephesians 1:10). But at the same time it has a personal, interior dimension which calls for a conversion of our personal attitudes and our scale of moral values. This raises the question of whether the Kingdom is primarily an exterior, sociological phenomenon or an interior, spiritual reality. Both views have found their supporters since the time of Jesus.

At the heart of the debate among Scripture scholars is the Greek word *entos* which is found in a reply by Jesus, quoted only in Luke (17:20-21):

> 'Some Pharisees asked Jesus when the Kingdom of God would come. His answer was: "The Kingdom of God does not come in such a way as to be seen. No one will say 'Look, here it is!' or 'There it is!' because the Kingdom of God is *entos* you" ...'

The Greek word *entos* can be translated in Hebrew as 'within' or as 'among' or 'in your midst'. (There are those who would argue from the context that the social meaning

149

is the correct interpretation because Jesus was answering a question posed to him by the Pharisees — surely the least likely people to be told that they had the right inner dispositions of the Kingdom — and the answer he gave is to a question about *when* the Kingdom would come, for which the latter meaning is the more likely answer. Other scholars counter this argument by saying that in the oral tradition Jesus' saying had an independent existence and that Luke decided to record it in the context of the Pharisees' question. The traditional translation of the Greek word *entos*, however, is 'within'.) Let us accept the ambiguity as indicating that both interpretations provide us with essential dimensions of the Kingdom. We will first see what is meant by the Kingdom as an inner, spiritual reality.

To enter into the fullness of the Kingdom, to become a conscious promoter of the Kingdom, it is not sufficient to know about it. Jesus did not come simply to impart information. Paul reminds us: 'The Kingdom of God is not a matter of words, but of power' (I Corinthians 4:20). He came to challenge us to become a new people, to be born again into the fullness of life. There is one word that keeps appearing in his announcement of the presence of the Kingdom: 'conversion' or 'repentence' or, as we have seen already, 'change your mind-set, live with a new consciousness'. In announcing the Kingdom, Jesus challenged, indeed reversed, the scale of values, the judgements, the attitudes of his contemporaries. In the Kingdom:

> The lowly are exalted and the mighty brought down (Luke 1:52).
> The poor, the children and the powerless are those who matter (Matthew 19:13-15).
> The first are last and the last first (Mark 10:31).
> The greatest becomes last and the servant of all (Mark 10:43-44).
> Dignity is in serving and not in being served. (Luke 22:24-27).

Anxiety for self-promotion is death and the gift of self is life (Mark 8:35).

And all this is summarised and fulfilled on the cross on which he who has, as St Paul expresses it, the nature of God, humbled himself and died the death of a slave, turning death into life and shame into glory (Philippians 2:6-9, John 17:5).

This call of Jesus to conversion was addressed to Jews and Gentiles alike, to all humanity. It was not a call to change religious affiliation: it was a challenge to a change of heart. Even though the Kingdom also has a social dimension and is about transforming society by bringing about new brother-sister relationships, no change in relationships is possible without a prior change of attitudes: a change from putting one's own interests before those of others. We are being reminded daily in our own environment, watching, or even involved in the continual industrial disputes between workers and management, that there is no perfect industrial structure, no perfect system of wage reform, no perfect scheme for social benefits that satisfies everyone. Every new system or structure is workable and acceptable only in so far as it is supported by the good will and generous attitude of those involved. The same must be said of the antagonisms within so many countries today: Afghanistan, Northern Ireland, Yugoslavia, Burundi and Rwanda, Sudan, Cyprus, North and South Korea, Sri Lanka, and others, including Jesus' own country Israel. No political settlement can last without a change of attitudes by individual citizens.

The Declaration of the Parliament of World Religions held in Chicago in 1993 contains the words: "Earth cannot be changed for the better unless the consciousness of individuals is changed first...Without risk and a readiness to sacrifice there can be no fundamental change in our situation".

The new scale of values proposed by Jesus for our more harmonious life and growth to wholeness will work only when the offer of new life made to each of us is accepted by the necessary act of 'con-version'. Systems and structures and institutions and customs only change because people change.

Conversion is, of its nature, personal, but that is not to say it is individualistic. In fact, conversion to the Kingdom which Jesus manifests is a conversion from a self-centred life to a community-oriented life. So the Kingdom also has a social, exterior dimension, as we shall be seeing in the next chapter. If people are to live by new values in their relationships with others, then this Kingdom which Jesus proclaimed appears as a new social and spiritual order. Jesus was a nonconformist, a sign of contradiction (Luke 2:34), denouncing the enslaving social and religious order of his day. 'You have heard how it was said to our ancestors ... but I say this to you ...' (Matthew 5:20-48). As might be expected, such confrontation created a crisis: 'So the people could not agree about him. Some would have liked to arrest him, but no one actually laid hands on him' (John 7:43-44). 'Then some of the Pharisees said "This man cannot be from God ..." And there was disagreement among them' (John 9:16).

Unity is the goal of the Kingdom, both internal unity (our achieving wholeness) and our social unity (through right relationships). The Christian understands our final destiny to be union with God, while Eastern religions understand our human destiny to be absorption into God. Both western and eastern religions are attempting to express the inexpressible. We agree on *what* our final human destiny is: no one knows just *how* it is to be accomplished.

The unity of the Kingdom is not a static unity but a creative unity, always creating a better future, a source of new energies and possibilities as the parables of the Leaven and the Mustard Seed so well describe.

But for us who are internally disintegrated and pulled in all directions by conflicting demands and pressures, the path to unity, both internal and collective, is one of pain.

Till the end of time, the fulfilment of God's creative vision — the realisation of the Kingdom — will be through confrontation and pain, through letting go and venturing out.

> 'Up to the present time all creation groans with pain like the pain of childbirth. But it is not just creation alone which groans; we who have the Spirit as the first of God's gifts also groan within ourselves, as we wait for God to make us his children and set our whole being free' (Romans 8:22-23).

8

THE KINGDOM
SHAPE OF SOCIETY

If the very essence of living by Kingdom values is to be conscious of the divine dimension in oneself, in other people and in all of nature, — as Karl Jung put it: 'the pattern of God exists in every man' — then acting upon that appreciation will govern all our relationships. As human beings, acknowledging that God is our common Father, our primary relationship among ourselves is that of sisterhood and brotherhood. This is the essence of living with Kingdom values. In the last chapter we saw that there is an outer, a social dimension to the Kingdom vision of Jesus as well as an inner, personal dimension. In this chapter we will look at the implications of the former which calls for a colossal paradigm shift in the way we order society.

So revolutionary is this shift which Jesus proposed, requiring a completely new social framework, that we are not surprised that only now, in our own time, after two thousand years, are we beginning to see the tiniest signs appear of a desire for change from a hierarchical-structured society to a community-structured society. However, it must be said that any plan to establish a Christian civilisation of the elect was entirely foreign to both Jesus and the early Christians. His vision was not that of a political theocracy for that was what already existed among the Jews and was precisely what Jesus was rejecting: the system by which some were 'in', 'belonged' (the pure) and some excluded (the unclean).

Wherever we human beings live together we need to form a social structure to regulate our relationships. This ranges from the family unit — whether nuclear or extended — to the village, town, state or nation. Each is a search for a perfect way to share life and our mutual dependence in peace and friendship. But because of our inability as ego-centred creatures to share life fully, openly — because we dare not take the risk of that — our relationships are strained by fear. We overcome our fear by dominating that which we fear. So our social structures, instead of being life-enhancing for everyone, become structures of oppression. Instead of giving a fuller life to others, we take life and freedom from others 'to keep them in their place'. We have only to look at our daily newspapers to be reminded of how domination gives birth to violence, whether it be the collective violence of a suppressed racial minority or the violence of frustrated individuals deprived of security, of a job prospect, of an opening to improve themselves. Our whole world economy is based upon the few dominating the many. Today we are seeing this on a global scale. Ten percent of the human population is classified as affluent, consuming more than three-quarters of the planet's resources, and will go to any lengths to keep it that way. The perpetuation of domination in our human society, since it is a power structure, is due to our failure to be fully human: our failure to love unconditionally.

As far back as we can trace in our western religious history —to Abraham's time, some 4,000 years ago — we already see society based on a pyramid or hierarchy model. But there is evidence that further back still it was not so. The hierarchy model, which is a male-dominated model, seems to have become the pattern when our ancestors took the evolutionary step from being hunter-gatherers to developing skills in agriculture and animal husbandry. The development of agriculture required more stable communities needing to possess land they could call their own and defend against invaders. Defence meant the need to fight. The need to fight required male warriors. The tribes that developed cattle breeding required more and more grazing land so unlike the settled farmers they became nomads. They too had their male warriors to conquer the pastures their cattle needed.

Between 4,300 and 2,800 BCE three major waves of nomadic cattle herders of Indo-European or Aryan-language-speaking stock swept down into Europe from the Asiatic and European north-east. Led by powerful priests and warriors they brought into Europe their male gods of war. What kind of society did they encounter, and gradually overturn? In her fascinating book *The Chalice and the Blade* Riane Eisler reports from her research that in the Neolithic period (10,000 - 4,000 BCE) our ancestors worshipped the creator as a goddess, one who gave fertility, and not as a male god. Consequently the feminine values of creativity and nurturing were uppermost over the male values of domination and rule by fear or threat. Eisler presents plenty of evidence that during this period people lived in a non-male-dominated, non-hierarchical society. Although it was a matrilinear

157

society, in which descent and inheritance were traced through the mother, it was not a female-dominated society. It was an egalitarian society in which women played key roles in all aspects of life. From the absence of any signs of heavy fortifications or throwing weapons belonging to this period we can deduce that it was a peace-loving society.

Another explanation of what brought about changed gender relations is proposed by Leonard Shlain in *The Alphabet versus the Goddess*. As his title hints, he proposes that it was the emergence of alphabetic literacy which fundamentally reconfigured the human brain. Shlain believes that agricultural preliterate cultures were principally informed by holistic right-brain modes that venerated the goddess and feminine values and images. The development of writing, particularly alphabets, drove cultures towards left-brain thinking. This initiated the decline of the feminine and ushered in the reign of patriarchy and misogyny. (I should add that his book ends on the optimistic note that today's proliferation of film, TV, graphics and computers is once again reconfiguring the brain by encouraging right-brain modes of thought and bringing about the re-emergence of the feminine!)

Ken Wilber in his *A Brief History of Everything* offers another explanation of how men came to dominate society. In what he calls the 'horticultural' period — farming with a hoe — the work of food production was done by women. They prayed to the goddess for fertility. With the advent of agriculture, — farming with the ox and plough, which he dates between 4,000 and 2,000 BCE, food production became male work. Men prayed and sacrificed to male gods. This advanced farming created over-production of food, which gave men leisure time for cultural pursuits (metal-work) and warfare. The first great military empires began around 3,000 BCE. But it gave them time too for more contemplative pursuits — writing, mathematics, philosophy — producing the great sages of what Karl Jaspers refers to as the Axial Period. In this period (approx. 600-300 BCE) were born most of the great religious traditions. It was in the Axial Period too that polytheism gave way to monotheism. The gods of the former were Earth gods because of our early ancestors' complete dependence on the earth to supply all the essentials for life. With monotheism the focus of religion moved from Earth to sky: from the Earth Mother to the distant Sky Father, and later, from the primitive Sky Father to our own 'Heavenly Father'. With this new focus the Earth was regarded as fallen, wicked, to be dominated and used, while it was the spiritual world of Heaven that was by contrast the all-important. So began the dichotomy between the 'natural' and the 'super-natural'.

Arnold Toynbee, studying world history, wrote in 1973:

> Some of the major maladies of the present day world — in particular the recklessly extravagant consumption of nature's irreplaceable treasures, and the pollution of those of them that man has not already devoured — can be traced back to a religious cause, and this cause is the rise of monotheism ... Monotheism, as enunciated in the book of Genesis, has removed the age-old restraint that was once placed on man's greed by his awe. Man's greedy impulse to exploit nature used to be held in check by his pious worship of nature.

Nearer home, hierarchy seems to have appeared among the Celts around 2,000 BCE, which was their Bronze Age. We find more respect being given to those who possessed weapons and jewellery: the wealthy people.

Thomas Berry, in *The Dream of the Earth*, names four patriarchal establishments 'that have been in control of Western history over the centuries': the classical empires, the ecclesiastical establishment, the nation-state and the modern (transnational) corporation. 'These four are exclusively male dominated and primarily for fulfilment in terms of the human as envisaged by men. Women had minimal if any consistent role in the direction of these establishments.'

It is difficult for us today to imagine how society can be ordered in any other than with a hierarchical shape. This is the shape it had in Jesus' day. His ancestors, the Semitic people who invaded Canaan from the South were also nomadic herdsmen ruled by warriors and priests, the Levites, and brought with them a male god of war: Jehovah or Yahweh. Chapter 21 of the Book of Numbers describes Yahweh's instructions to Moses for a war of revenge against the Midianites. Yahweh gave clear instructions about the distribution of booty between the soldiers, the priests and the community (in that order of importance). Eisler writes: 'The one thing they [the invaders] all had in common was a dominator model of social organisation: a social system in which male dominance, male violence and a generally hierarchic and authoritarian social structure was the norm'. They put a higher value on the power that takes life than on the power that gives life.

Given this social structure in Israel two thousand years ago, it is understandable why the Christ had to appear among us as Jesus the male rather than in a feminine role.

OF DIVINE ORIGIN?

It is sometimes argued that we were created to be hierarchy creatures; that the structure is born from the struggle for the power which we feel is necessary to

160

survive in society. The argument is based upon observations made of the animal kingdom. Take, for example, the chimpanzee, a native of Central Africa. Chimpanzees are one of the four great apes (with gorillas, orangutans and gibbons) but closer to us than the others. The ape family split off from our own branch of the evolutionary tree. We can call them our 'cousins' since we have 98.5% of our DNA in common. (What a difference 1.5% can make!) We observe that chimpanzees have their own pecking order which is respected when it comes to rivalry for the leadership of their extended family. So is the hierarchy pattern in our genes?

Others argue that the hierarchy paradigm is of divine origin because the source of all power is God and God is 'above' creation. But then we have to ask, what is the origin of that belief? Which came first, the notion that God is 'above' and outside creation and that therefore perfection and power must be at the pyramid's peak, or did the human creation of the hierarchy structure cause humanity to conclude that God must be 'at the top'?

We have to remember that the creation accounts of Jewish mythology, in which the pyramid structure is already in evidence, were written only a few hundred years before Jesus, by which time the Chosen People had already experienced being structured into a hierarchical society with a king at the top, a king of divine choice. By that time they were city-dwellers, male-dominated, belligerent — (we read in I Chronicles 20:1, 'In the Spring, at the time of the year when kings usually go to war ...') — the men had gained ascendancy over women and the rational mind had come to dominate the intuitive. It does not surprise us then to read in the very first chapter in Genesis of an external God, powerful, who creates 'man' and then creates a woman out of a part of man, a woman who is reported to be the one tempted by an evil serpent and responsible for 'the Fall'. It shows how much female creative power had become debased. We read of God saying: 'Now we will make human beings; they will be like us and resemble us. They will have *power* over the fish, the birds and all animals, domestic and wild, large and small' and later on instructing Adam and Eve to 'fill the Earth and *conquer* it'. This was a human projection onto God as creator, of the social structure that was already in place. Sadly, it is upon this biblical base that we of the Western religions, acknowledging Abraham as our common father, have given ourselves authority to dominate, to use for our benefit, to destroy even, all the rest of creation at our whim. We still speak of 'the conquest of nature'. Incidentally, having dominion over the animals (Genesis 1:26) did not include killing them for food (1:29). That permission is given only later (9:3) to Noe.

The hierarchical paradigm is not of divine origin but is a human construct upon which divine authority has been bestowed. Once a power structure pertains — and hierarchy is all about the possession and use of power — a power grading takes place. Absolute power is at the pinnacle and trickles downwards, the powerless being 'at the bottom of the stack'. It demands obedience to the level above and assumes domination over the level below. It is a structure of control. It breeds fear, fear of failure, and is therefore the enemy of risking anything new.

In the Judeo-Christian tradition (and in most other cultures) men are above women while children are beneath adults, with adults owning and controlling children; the fit are held to be of more value than the disabled. It appears that in the eyes of the medical profession, when a choice of whom to treat has to be made, the life of an old person is judged less valuable than that of a person with many years ahead of them. The worth of each is measured by their value to society which in turn is measured by their achievement. How many women still describe their role in life as 'I'm only a housewife'. The role of women in the home has no value by the achievement measurement.

Hierarchy is the tool used to conserve order. Two obvious examples of this are the army and the Church, in both of which order is considered to be essential.

The hierarchy model has been evident in the Church ever since its earliest years when Church structure modelled itself on the Roman Empire. In fact the very word 'hier-archy' was coined by Dionysius, a 6th century monk in Syria, to denote the totality of ruling persons in the Church. Hier-archy means sacred government and we speak of those with power in ecclesiastical society, the Bishops, as 'The Hierarchy', from whom instructions, doctrines and precepts filter down. Church leaders have developed theories and theologies to justify their privileged position.

One of the most powerful arguments against Christianity, Bishop Richard Holloway reminded us in a Christmas-eve BBC broadcast in 2000, is that for most of its history the Church has lent its support to whatever system was on top and supported it. It preached resignation, not revolt. Slaves were told to be good slaves content with their lot; women were told not to upset their husbands and always do what they were told. It preached self- denial to the people at the bottom in order to justify the privileges of those at the top.

THE JESUS MODEL

But Jesus proposed a different model. His ideal for humanity was radical. He was able to envisage how it could be otherwise. Sadly though, only a few years after Pentecost, Jesus' small group of followers were so unable to situate themselves in another social shape than that around them that they began to organise their converts on the pattern of the contemporary civil state and themselves to assume the role in the new community that the Pharisees and Sadducees were playing in the Jewish nation.

But this is not how it is to be in the Kingdom. Jesus cut right through the traditions of his society and in doing so challenged people — and us — to see that there is another way of ordering our relationships.

Nowhere in the Gospels do we find Jesus approving the hierarchy model. Quite the contrary, as we see in the instruction he gave to those who were to be leaders in his new community:

> 'You know that the men who are considered to be rulers of the heathen have power over them, and the leaders have complete authority. This, however, is not the way it is among you. If one of you wants to be great, he must be the servant of the rest; and if one of you wants to be first, he must be the slave of all. For even the Son of Man did not come to be served; he came to serve' (Mark 10:42-45).

This was said to them after they had been prospecting for positions in the Kingdom of glory. The only occasion when Jesus allowed the crowd to proclaim him as a king was immediately preceding his being tortured and put to death. The crowd cheered and waved palm branches as he entered Jerusalem. And even then he did not ride triumphantly on a horse like a conquering king, but on a donkey, the peasants' beast of burden.

Hierarchy values us for what we *have* or for what we can contribute from what we have: our role, our abilities, our leadership skills, our honours and titles, our education, our class or caste. In such a paradigm we are what we are only by being measured against others. Our worth, even in our own eyes — our self-worth — depends upon how others regard us. This breeds the ethos of competition. By contrast the community paradigm (as I shall call that demanded by the Kingdom vision) values us for what we *are*. It is non-competitive. Our worth comes from our being of value to and beloved by God, because there is that of God in us. We are acceptable because we are a brother or sister of the same Father.

The parable of the wedding feast (Matthew 22:2-10) in which the king's servants are sent out into the streets to invite just anyone in to sit at the same table — female and male, married and unmarried, slave and free, pure and impure, rich and poor — reveals Jesus' radical egalitarianism in which discrimination and social position no longer have a place.

When mothers brought children to Jesus, his bodyguard scolded them, as much as to say: 'Jesus has more important people to bless and heal than mere children'. But we are told that Jesus was angry with his disciples and what he said about the Kingdom of God being as much for children as for adults reveals again that he did not judge a person's worth by their place in society (Mark 10:13-16). He had no time for the pomp of the 'teachers of the law and the Pharisees'. To the crowds as well as to his disciples he said:

> 'They love the best places at feasts and the reserved seats in the synagogues; they love to be greeted with respect in the market places and to be called 'Teacher'. You must not be called 'Teacher', because you are all brothers of one another and have only one Teacher. And you must not call anyone here on earth 'Father', because you have only the one Father in heaven. Nor should you be called 'Leader' because your one and only leader is the Messiah' (Matthew 23: 6-10).

165

The father figure in the family of his time — and still in most societies today — represented patriarchy, male supremacy. Notice how Jesus, by reserving the name Father for God alone, subverts all patriarchal structures. 'Whoever does what God wants him to do is my brother, my sister, my mother' (Mark 3:35). No father mentioned! In Mark 10:29-30 'Anyone who leaves home or brothers or sisters or mother or father or children or fields for me and for the gospel, will receive much more in this present age. He will receive a hundred times more houses, brothers, sisters, mothers, children and fields' — but not fathers!

In a parable Jesus has the master turn servant: 'How happy are those servants whose master finds them awake and ready when he returns. I tell you, he will take off his cloak, ask them to sit down and will wait on them' (Luke 12:37).

Later, Jesus was to turn his words into action to illustrate the form he expected leadership to take in the Kingdom community. While at supper with his disciples 'he rose from the table, took off his outer garment and tied a towel around his waist. Then he poured some water into a basin and began to wash the disciples' feet and dry them with the towel round his waist'. Peter objected at seeing his Master performing the action of a servant. 'After Jesus had washed their feet, he put his outer garment back on and returned to his place at the table. "Do you understand what I have just done to you?" he asked. "You call me master and Lord and it is right that you do so, because it is what I am. I, your Lord and Master, have just washed your feet. You then should wash one another's feet. I have set an example for you, so that you will do just what I have done for you"' (John 13:4-15).

It was on another occasion at table that 'Jesus noticed how some of the guests were choosing the best places, so he told this parable to all of them: "When someone invites you to a wedding feast, do not sit down in the best place. It could happen that someone more important than you has been invited ... instead, when you are invited go and sit in the lowest place ... for everyone who makes himself great will be humbled, and everyone who humbles himself will be made great"' (Luke 14:7-ll).

Contrary to the prevailing custom Jesus did not treat women as being in any way inferior to men. He had special concern for the marginalised, the outcasts, for lepers, for the public sinners, for the despised tax-collectors. Roles played no part in the way he valued people. The Pharisees recognised this. When sent to challenge Jesus they began with: 'We know that you tell the truth, without worrying about what people think. A man's rank means nothing to you...' (Mark 12:14).

Although he understood his mission to be only to his own people — 'I have been sent only to the lost sheep, the people of Israel' (Matthew 15:24) — and believed 'It is from the Jews that salvation comes' (John 4:22), he did not regard his own Chosen People to be superior to others. He praised the faith of the Canaanite woman who begged for her daughter to be healed (Matthew 15:21-28), he did the same when the Roman centurion asked Jesus to heal his servant (Luke 7:9), he spoke at length to the Samaritan woman at the well in Sychar (John 4:7-26) when all Samaritans were shunned by orthodox Jews as heretics.

In the hierarchy paradigm we give greater credence when a person is thought 'to speak with authority', because of their position in society's pecking order. Jesus was often asked by what authority he said the outrageous things people heard. But he never replied directly to that question. The authenticity of what he said — people just knew at their deepest level that what he said was right —

gave it its own authority. It matched their experience: it 'rang true'.

CRACKS ARE APPEARING

And now, two thousand years on, we see encouraging signs that humanity is taking small steps to move from a hierarchy society to a community society.

In Chapter 1 we listed just some of the character-istics of today's shift in consciousness. We asked how they should be understood, and promoted (or not) by a Christian. We needed to match them against Jesus' vision of the Kingdom. In the light of what we have said above about the structure of society — how it is now and how it might be if it were more in accord with the Jesus vision — let us look at six contemporary signs which, I suggest, reveal that a paradigm shift is beginning to come about which favours the Kingdom becoming a reality.

The hierarchy structure is a structure of command: the domination of some requiring the obedience of others. Obedience to authority was drummed into us from our earliest years. God, or God's word in the Bible understood literally as eternally binding, was invoked as the source of all authority. 'To be disobedient is to sin' we were told. This presupposed an 'outside' God who had created a 'designer' world in which all was pre-determined. Anyone who tried to suggest that moral laws might change with time and circumstance, with new discoveries and deeper insights, was accused of 'playing God'.

But today, for a whole variety of reasons, the authority of those 'in authority' is questioned. Just because a person is a teacher or a parent or a priest or a politician it does not follow that we owe them blind obedience. A more highly educated population asks questions, wants to make its own responsible decisions, needs to challenge the assumptions of 'leaders'. Young people are no longer willing to give docile obedience to father-figures unless such a person's authority is felt to be authentic, by which they mean that it is authenticated by their own experience. People world-wide are no longer happy to have others decide their future or their children's future, but want to have a say in it themselves. Witness the universal move towards democracy.

Secondly, there is currently a reaction against male domination and a desire for women and men to have equal opportunities. This is as true in the Church as it is in the professions. Traditional roles are even being reversed, often for economic reasons: the man becomes the house-husband while the woman is the bread-winner. In society at large, men are no longer automatically awarded a position above women. But there is something deeper at play than the liberalising of women. It is the appreciation of what we have come to call the feminine values —intuition, creativity, compassion, nurturing — and the desire that they, along with the masculine values, need to be in balance in every human being, irrespective of gender.

A PROGRESSION TOWARDS HUMAN RIGHTS

Thirdly, there is growing concern throughout the world for 'human rights'. Respect for the individual's worth is a preliminary step towards forming a communitarian society in which everyone's intrinsic worth is valued. We are familiar with that Declaration of Human Rights that was made during the French Revolution of the late 18th century calling for 'Liberty, Equality, Fraternity'. The very idea, which we regard as quite normal today, struck fear into the political and ecclesiastical leaders at the time.

Pope Pius VI (1775-1799) strongly condemned this manifesto of the Revolution. As late as 1864 the Vatican published a 'Syllabus of Errors', mentioning socialism as one of them and concluding with: 'It is an error to claim that the Roman Pontiff can and ought to reconcile himself with progress, with liberalism and with modern civilisation'.

We witness the progression of waves towards personal freedom if we list the series of emancipations in our recent history: absolute monarchy being replaced by democracy, emancipation from slavery, the emancipation of women from male domination (claiming the right to possess property, to have a vote, to enjoy social equality and to have equal career opportunities). The emancipation of children from child labour, — the boy chimney sweeps — at least in the West. The emancipation of colonies from foreign imperialism, of coloured races from white supremacy, and more recently of homosexuals from heterosexual righteousness. Each emancipation has been a struggle against the fierce resistance of those wishing to maintain the contemporary pattern of society.

This concern throughout the world for 'human rights' is the acknowledgement of the innate value of every human being. Within recent decades we have had the publication of a Universal Declaration of Human Rights (1948) and indeed the creation of a body able to draw up and have the authority to publish such a document: the United Nations, witnessing our world-wide interdependence. Some have regarded this document as the expression of God's Will for our own time, spelling out as it does, the deepest aspirations of the human heart for the well-being of all humanity.

There is a long list of Non-Governmental Organisations (NGOs) and Aid Agencies concerned with justice issues, not forgetting the innumerable smaller groups giving voice to the struggle of particular ethnic minorities. Such concerns as the elimination of Third World Debt stir hundreds of thousands of us into action with the conviction that each one of us can make a difference, each has a contribution to make towards bettering this world.

But the demand for the rights of every individual is only the first step towards the community structure. Now we need a Universal Declaration of Human Duties! When everyone has a sense of their duty to others, the rights of each will automatically be respected. Rights breed individualism: duties breed community.

CHANGE ORIGINATES AT THE GRASS ROOTS

Fourthly, the initiative for change for better is no longer expected to filter down from on high. Change is born at the grassroots and what is giving power to this source of change today is 'networking'. The power to forge our future lies in the large number of ordinary people with their inventiveness and enthusiasm pooling their ideas and resources by networking. This is 'people power'. This is given a reinforcement, a new ability, in our own time with the rapid spread of the 'World Wide Web'. The Internet is a tremendous equaliser. It ignores time and distance. Anyone, anywhere, with no need to advertise their 'authority' can post their point of view on everyone else's screen. There is no controlling parent figure to censor or disapprove. By networking, power is exercised horizontally. This is the new force shaping world opinion and bringing about change.

A number of initiatives have sprung up from the grassroots in recent years to counter the domination of the prevailing economic system. They put people and the environment at the centre of economic thinking. Such initiatives as the New Economics Foundation (founded by the leaders of the 1984 Other Economic Summit — TOES — which challenged the G7 Summit). Local Exchange Trading Systems (LETS) allow members to trade goods and services without using conventional money but using a local credit or 'currency'. Starting with four in 1990 there are now over three hundred LETS groups in Britain with 22,000 people signed up. Time Dollars, pioneered in the United States of America, is similar: local people form a system whereby participants earn credits for performing services. More recently Time Banks have been launched in Britain — over 30 are up and running — which work on the same principle. One hour of your time given in some form of service to another entitles you to an hour of their time. Time is the criterion of value. These schemes are based on the philosophy that all work is of equal value, whether cleaning the office or managing it, because the value lies in the person doing the work and not in the product. They are de-linking value from monetary price, demonstrating that money does not define the limits of what is possible.

The New Economics Foundation publishes a guide entitled *Community Works* listing thirty-seven grassroots initiatives of a wide range of community economic actions.

GLOBALISATION

Globalisation accounts for another crack in the hierarchy paradigm. The word was first used in the context of a global economy but it now encompasses the great new phenomenon of our time, the integration of all aspects of life into one world-wide network. So we need to distinguish between globalisation in its broadest sense, the world become a global village, and corporate globalisation. Whereas the latter is a trade and financed based strategy by which transnational companies strive for world-wide economic power through such bodies as the World Trade Organisation, the former embodies a spiritual dimension. It is with this latter that we are concerned here because it can be understood as a movement towards the fulfilment of that unity of all humanity for which Jesus prayed. For instance, we in the West are becoming more aware of the richness and holiness of the followers of Eastern religions — Hinduism, Buddhism, Sikhism — who now live among us. We are more aware of how their particular insights into the spiritual journey can enrich our own under-standing of Christian revelation.

Or again, we witness a new political force arising alongside government, traditional political parties and trade unions and it is named 'Civil Society'. It is a conglomerate of ordinary folk, groups of marginalised people, environmentalists, ecologists, discontented socialists and a wide variety of pressure groups: all those who are reacting against the adverse consequences of an unbridled free market economy that threatens the quality of human lives. One such is an anti-globalisation movement setting out its position in a letter 'Our World is Not for Sale', launched in Geneva in 2001 and already hundreds of organisations in countries all over the world have signed up to it.

Despite all the negative issues that are laid at globalisation's door, like the eclipse of particular cultures by a new global culture, it does mark the end of the supremacy of the Christian West. Although numerically there are more Christians in the southern hemisphere

173

today than in the northern, culturally Christianity has always been western and western culture over the last two millennia has been Christian. The certainties that underpinned western society, that gave it the moral right to attempt to colonise the rest of the world, derived from belief in the unchangeable values of the Bible. But cultural Christianity is at an end. Different expressions of Christian ways of living are emerging from the grassroots (for example, through the methodology of Liberation Theology) and the days of a vertical form of ecclesiastical authority — even Vatican centralisation — are numbered.

The ideal is for all of humanity to order its life together by Kingdom values, ordered by interior, spiritual power rather than by external human-controlled power. Some see this as taking the form of a restored medieval Christendom, or universal membership of the Church. But with a Kingdom vision, not a Church vision, we can see this coming about under another or several titles, other than the Christian Church. No Kingdom values are so particular, so unique, that they are not found in other religions. Kingdom values are human values when a person is living by the highest values of humanity, to our full potential, living the life we were created to live.

And lastly, our hierarchy paradigm is being threatened by the realisation that as humans we do not, cannot, dominate Planet Earth: we are not outside and above it, a notion based on the idea of a God outside and above the Universe and that we humans are 'made in the image of God'. We can no longer claim superiority on our being the centre of and reason for all creation. In terms of the entire Universe, with its billions of known galaxies, this is absurd. The Incarnation, as it is understood by Christians, is in terms of Planet Earth. And

174

the place of humanity on Earth is very recent, very tiny and very destructive. Earth is our playground but we take our games too seriously. The fact that we believe the human being to be eternal does not diminish the value of the rest of our galaxy because it is temporal.

NEW FORMS OF LEADERSHIP

If the hierarchical pattern is slowly dissolving into a community-based pattern, it will inevitably mean a change in the way leadership is exercised: no longer from the top down. The new paradigm brings about a new appreciation of the purpose of 'authority': not to dominate but to facilitate, to enable each person to be creative, to accomplish, to grow. Underlying this is the realisation that my talents are not for my glory but for the common good.

Our present leadership pattern puts great reliance on a strong father/teacher figure 'at the top'. Eighty per cent of initiatives are taken by the leader, only twenty per cent by the community. This perpetuates the world of our childhood when we looked for security in a parent figure. As humanity reaches an adolescent stage — that of seeking self-identity, being led by ideals, becoming more self-assured — the leader is regarded more as an elder brother/sister in the community, taking the role of animator or co-ordinator.

With the community reaching maturity it is acknowledged that no one person is good at everything all the time. Because each person's talents are recognised, leadership is able to move round the community depending upon the task to be fulfilled and who is regarded as the best co-ordinator for this particular project. The leader of the moment is one among others but given a particular, temporary role. When creativity is shared, new ideas are not a threat.

It was this liberating of individuals to grow to their full stature, and to live in the sort of society that would make this possible, that was the Kingdom vision of which Jesus dreamed. His dream was not a sudden insight. The vision evolved from his and our religious history, and will continue to evolve. This is the subject of the next chapter which gives an overview of this history.

9

THE EVOLUTION OF
THE KINGDOM VISION

It seems so long ago since Jesus burst into human history with his revolutionary idea of a New Era which he was convinced God intends should be the mode of our life today, and so little appears to have happened to bring about any momentous change in the two thousand intervening years, that we can be forgiven for not appreciating that the Christ-time we live in is really a very recent era in human history. The author of the Letter to the Hebrews reminds us: '...he has made his appearance ... now at the end of the last age ...' (9.26). To understand this better, we need to put the Kingdom vision into historical perspective.

When the author of the Letter to the Ephesians writes of God's 'secret plan he had already decided to complete by means of the Christ' and explains that plan by saying: 'even before the world was made, God had already chosen us to be his through our union with the Christ' (1:3-10), he is saying that from the moment of humanity's first appearance on Earth — the current estimates of palaeontologists range from half a million to four million years ago — we were set on a journey towards 'the full stature of the Christ'. Within a time span of even half a million years, the arrival of Jesus as the Christ on the scene a mere two thousand years ago is a very recent event indeed. Why, we may ask, did it not happen sooner? Why had humanity to wait hundreds of thousands of years before we could learn what God's purpose is for our destiny, or be empowered to make a quantum leap into the New Era which heralds its fulfilment? Our first response must surely be one of immense gratitude that we find ourselves living in the Christ era, the era in which is proclaimed 'his message which is the secret he hid from all past ages but has now revealed to his people' (Colossians 1:26). We can only assume that the human race required a process of growth in consciousness before it was sufficiently evolved to be able to comprehend and accept the news that Jesus proclaimed.

We can speak of three major eras in this development of consciousness concerning God's purpose, and of course they cover very recent history — a mere four thousand years. We can also speak of them as the three eras of the Kingdom, since the Kingdom is the fulfilment of God's design which has been unfolding ever since the Big Bang (see the chart on the next page) though explicitly only with the appearance of Jesus. It was he, in speaking of a final judgement, who referred to 'the Kingdom which has been prepared for you ever since the creation of the world' (Matthew 25:34). We will look at each of these eras in turn. I call them:

— The period of the Israelites (The Old Testament period).
— The period of Jesus and his disciples.
— The period of Kingdom-Church identity.

We are now entering a fourth period, that leading to the New Era of the Spirit.

It will be noticed that the last two periods are related to the history of Christianity. This is not to say that the

The evolution of God's creative intent

The following Time chart is drawn from "THE UNIVERSE STORY" by Brian Swimme and Thomas Berry and from 'THE WEB OF LIFE - A NEW SYNTHESIS OF MIND AND MATTER' by Fritjof Capra.

All dates should be considered to be approximate.

15 billion years ago	The universe begins as a stupendous energy release. The original universe activity evolves into the gravitational, strong nuclear, weak nuclear and electromagnetic interactions. Before a millionth of a second has passed, the particles stabilise. The primal nuclei form within the first few minutes. As the universe becomes transparent, hydrogen and helium come forth.
10-14 billion years ago	The universe breaks into galactic clouds. The primal stars appear. The first elements are forged in the stars. The first supernovas give rise to second and third generation stars. Giant galaxies evolve by swallowing smaller galaxies.
5 billion years ago	A disc-like cloud floats in the Orion arm of the Milky Way Galaxy.
4.6 billion years ago	The star Tiamat explodes as a supernova providing the elements that will become the sun and the planets.
4.5 billion years ago	The Sun is born.
4.45 billion years ago	The Planets are formed, earth a fireball of cooling molten lava.
4 billion years ago	Earth brings forth atmosphere, condensation of steam form oceans and continents. The earth is submitted to thousands of years of lightning storms.

LIFE ON EARTH

3.5 billion years ago	The right conditions being available the first bacterial cell without nucleus arise.
2.5 billion years ago	Cells achieve photosynthesis, fermentation, sensing devises, and trading of genes. Continents stabilise.
2.3 billion years ago	The first ice ages.
2.2 billion years ago	The first nucleated cell.
2 billion years ago	Oxygen builds up in the atmosphere threatening all life.
1.8 billion years ago	A cell learns to deal with oxygen and proliferates.
1.5 billion years ago	Earth's surface and atmosphere established.
1.2 billion years ago	Locomotion becomes possible.
1 billion years ago	A cell invents sexual reproduction.
700 million years ago	The first multicellular creatures appear.
600 million years ago	Jellyfish, sea pens, flat worms.
500 million years ago	Early plants.
400 million years ago	Jawed fish. Land animals. Insects.
300 million years ago	Dinosaurs.
200 million years ago	Mammals.
100 million years ago	Flowering plants. First primates.
35 million years ago	Monkeys.
20 million years ago	Apes.
10 million years ago	Great apes.
4 million years ago	Upright walking australopithecus afarensis (southern apes) on the African Continent.
2.5 million years ago	Evidence of several australopithecus species.
2 million years ago	Homo habilis (skilful human).
1.6 million years ago	Homo erectus (upright human).
1 million years ago	Homo erectus settles in Asia.
400,000 years ago.	Homo erectus settles in Europe.
250,000 years ago	First evidence of homo sapiens (wise human).
125,000 years ago	Archaic forms of homo from homo sapiens. Homo erectus becomes extinct.
60,000 years ago	Homo neanderthalensis.
40,000 years ago	Homo sapiens fully evolved in Africa and Asia. Evidence of ritual burials.
35,000 years ago	Homo neanderthalensis. Homo sapiens fully evolved in Europe and settles in Australia.
20,000 years ago	Homo neanderthalensis extinct. Homo sapiens, only remaining human species, settles in America.
18,000 years ago	Spears, bows and arrows. Cave paintings.
11,000 years ago	Settled farming communities.
6000 years ago	Emergence of great civilisations. Writing. Wheel.
4000 years ago	World population 5-10 million.
2000 years ago	Birth of Jesus. Population 300 million.
Today	Population 6 billion.

Kingdom was not evolving in other areas of the world and through other major religions implicitly, but here we are observing its growth within the Christian tradition which alone gives it an explicit expression.

THE PERIOD OF THE ISRAELITES

There was one characteristic by which the Israelites were culturally different from the tribes which surrounded them. Most of the other peoples around Palestine, including the great cultures of Egypt, Mesopotamia and Greece, understood their existence in terms of life cycles. As day follows night, so season follows season and generations give way to generations through cycles of birth, growth, decline and death, then reincarnation: an endless cycle of events manipulated by various gods. But the Israelites had a different view of life. The extraordinary events whereby, against enormous odds, they were delivered under the leadership of Moses from their life of slavery to the Egyptians caused them to reflect on the hand of God in their history. Unlike the gods of neighbouring civilisations, their Yahwah seemed to be constantly opening new doors to them, leading them to greater and greater self-determination and unification of the tribes that made up their race. The more they reflected upon the events of their history, the more they understood God's hand in them. For the Israelites, life was not lived in a closed circle but there was a direction to it. It seemed to be progressing somewhere. Hebrew consciousness of a direction began with the Exodus, with the creation of Israel as a people. At first this consciousness grew as an oral tradition, passed down by word of mouth from one generation to the next. Then, after the Chosen People had settled in the Promised Land, this tradition began to be written down, over a long period, by a variety of authors in a variety of styles and often with exaggeration to emphasise some events as 'miraculous'. This is the collection of writings that is known as the Hebrew Scriptures or what Christians call the Old Testament.

The Israelites were a people with a past, a history, through which they could interpret God as leading them. They were a people who had a future. They looked forward to the moment when God would send a Messiah, a Saviour, among them, though as we have seen, their expectations of a Messiah differed between different groups.

During the two thousand years of the Israelites' recorded history —since God promised Abraham 'I will give you many descendants, and they will become a great nation' (Genesis 12:1-2) — their consciousness developed by a process of deeper and deeper understanding of God's ways and of his plan for them.

Over periods of wandering as nomads to find their identity, of settling in a land they could call their own, of choosing to be led by human kings, of localising God's presence among them in the Temple, of being purified through conquest and exile, their awareness of God and their relationship to God was gradually refined. First from an idea of many gods, to the notion that theirs was the supreme God, to an understanding that there is only one God.

Similarly, their moral code became more refined. Take just one example: the path from vengeance to forgiveness. We read in Genesis that Lamech boasted to his wives:

> 'I have killed a young man because he struck me. If seven lives are taken for killing Cain, seventy-seven will be taken if anyone kills me' (4:23-24).

Moses was much more moderate. He proposed that vengeance should not exceed the offence: 'an eye for an eye and a tooth for a tooth, hand for hand, foot for foot...' (Exodus 21:23-25). As Moses' followers entered the land of Canaan they became more lenient, at least to those who injured another by accident. They named six 'cities of refuge' none being more than thirty kilometres away from any village. Any Israelite killing someone by accident could run there to be tried. If found innocent, he was protected. As the Israelites grew to understand that their God was a forgiving God, they realised that the same was expected of them. Then the question arose as to how often one was expected to forgive. In the time of Jesus it was generally accepted that one should forgive three times. It was this question that Peter put to Jesus and received the reply: 'seventy times seven': in other words, every time, without limit (Matthew 18:21-22). Forgive four hundred and ninety times and it becomes a habit!

Until humanity had evolved to a certain point of consciousness, the revelation of Jesus would have met with complete incomprehension. 'We were slaves of the ruling spirits of the universe before we reached spiritual maturity. But when the right time finally came, God sent his own son' (Galatians 4:3-4). It does not require a great deal of honesty on our part to admit that two thousand years later there are very few people on Earth who have really grasped the full impact of Jesus' Good News and are able to live by his values. The vast majority of us are still more akin to pre-Jesus people in the way in which we relate to God and to each other. The Kingdom has hardly begun to burst forth!

THE PERIOD OF JESUS AND HIS DISCIPLES

This is the shortest but by far the most important period: that in which Jesus lived among us both to enlighten us about our glorious destiny and to empower us to break through to a totally new way of living. 'Your hearts and minds must be made completely new, and you must put on the new self, which is created in God's likeness and reveals itself in the true life that is upright and holy' (Ephesians 4:23-24). How easily we fail to notice and so fail to be inspired by the 'newness' of the life Jesus offers us and the enormity of the transition from the former life to the latter. As a consequence we fail to tap the power given us by the Christ to take that leap forward.

Jesus' own audience was made up of Jews, and the band of men he called around him were Jews too. We have already seen that Jesus, in speaking of the Kingdom, was speaking of a reality much broader than was understood by his contemporaries: a Kingdom which was not the restoration of Israel as an independent nation, but the universal brother/sisterhood of humanity; a Kingdom which though not political was both social and interior. He did not intend his Kingdom to spawn a new religion, nor for his followers to forsake their Judaic cultural home, as happened with the later birth of 'Christianity' as a new religion over against other philosophies of life.

Jesus formed a group around him, a community of disciples, who by their manner of living and their message, were to aid him in his mission of making the Christ era a reality. It was as simple as that. They were in fact called 'The Way' and were regarded in the period following Pentecost as yet another sub-group of Jewish religious life, as were the Pharisees, the Sadducees, the Essenes, the Zealots, the Qumran community. Jesus asked for no new form of worship, so his followers continued with their Jewish worship, going to the Temple in Jerusalem each day for prayer (Acts 3:1); they observed the Jewish diets (Acts 10:14), continued to circumcise their sons (Acts 21:21) and announced the Good News of Jesus to synagogue congregations on the Sabbath (Acts 9:20). They did not see themselves as any different from their co-religionists except that they saw in Jesus the promised Messiah and were convinced that through him a new era of their history had begun. They were what today we call 'fulfilled Jews'. When an angel released the apostles from jail it instructed them: 'Go and stand in the Temple, and tell the people all about this new life' (Acts 5:20). As these Messianic Jews later found themselves among Gentile people, their leaders came to realise that they had a mission beyond Palestine; that this new way of living was equally valid for all people by virtue, not of their religious background, but of their humanity. With the destruction by the Romans of Jerusalem and of the second Temple in 70 CE, the followers of The Way fled from their homeland and made a cultural leap out of Judaism. This was when the Jesus movement began to take on all the trappings of a religion.

THE PERIOD OF KINGDOM-CHURCH IDENTITY

The enormity of this leap taken by the small new Jewish sect out of Palestine onto the stage of the then known world, is easily overlooked. For one thing, as we noticed in the last chapter, it would seem that Jesus himself had not foreseen that his proposed new way of living and relating should reach beyond the Jewish nation (Matthew 15:24). Jesus exhorted his contemporaries to become better Jews, to fulfil the Law of Moses. 'Do not think that I have come to do away with the Law of Moses and the teachings of the prophets. I have not come to do away with them, but to make their teachings come true' (Matthew 5:17).

When a pagan woman from Syro-Phoenecia begged him for a cure for her daughter he replied: 'I have been sent only to those lost sheep, the people of Israel'. He did in fact grant her request because he was so amazed at her faith. (Matthew 15:21-28). He was culturally conditioned to believe that God's blessings came only through the Jewish race. 'It is from the Jews that salvation comes', he is reported as saying (John 4:22). Incidents such as the faith of the Syro-phoenecian woman and the Roman centurian (Luke 7:1-10) were a multi-racial lesson for him.

When Jesus sent out his twelve followers to prepare the ground for him, he instructed them: 'Do not go to any Gentile territory or any Samaritan towns. Instead, you are to go to those lost sheep, the people of Israel' (Matthew 10:5-6).

True, there are other verses in Matthew's Gospel (10:18, 24:14, 28:19) which would seem to indicate that Jesus was expecting his disciples to preach to the Gentile world too. But we must remember that the Gospels were written years after 'The Way' had spread into Asia Minor and it is quite likely that they are not the literal words of Jesus but a post-Pentecost interpretation of his mission. It would appear from what we read in the Letter to the Ephesians that it was under the inspiration of the Holy Spirit at Pentecost that the Apostles learned that their mission was to extend beyond the People of Israel:

> In past times mankind was not told this secret, but God has revealed it *now by the Spirit* to his holy apostles and prophets. The secret is that by means of the Gospel the Gentiles have a part with the Jews in God's blessings; they are members of

the same body and share in the promise that God made through Jesus the Christ' (3:5-6).

The move into the Gentile world had a number of universally important consequences for the next 2,000 years, not only for Christianity itself but for all who came under Christianity's influence over the two millennia.

There was the growing realisation among Jesus' followers that the 'Second Coming' or 'Final Coming' of the Christ and the end of the world was not as immediate as at first thought. St Paul makes this clear in his second letter to the Thessalonians (2:2-3), a letter written to correct the views he expressed in his first letter to them (4:15-5:11). As this truth dawned upon these early followers, they began to understand themselves to be the 'Body of Christ', the new presence of the Christ in the world. As Jesus had made the Kingdom a reality by living as a Kingdom person, so they, as the group formed by Jesus, became identified with the Kingdom. As they called themselves the 'Ekklesia' (Church) to emphasise their break with the synagogue, all that Jesus had said about the Kingdom was interpreted as being said about the Church. Since the loaded Jewish phrase 'Kingdom of God' would have had little meaning to Greek-culture Christians, the expression was rarely used in the speeches and writings of the apostles.

As the community grew in numbers and in geographical extent, it became institutionalised and began to show the characteristics of an organised religion. In the first place, it formalised its own way of worship. With the Temple destroyed, there was no holy place for worship. The simple gathering of followers meeting to break bread together in their homes and celebrate the continuing presence of the Lord in their midst, became a cultic act which included the synagogue liturgy.

Secondly, the simplicity of the announcement of Good News encountered the Greek world of philosophers, where it became intellectualised. The Lutheran theologian Adolf von Harnack has summed up this development: 'When the Messiah became Logos the Gospel became Theology'. As the years went by and the message spread it became necessary to write down different accounts of Jesus' life and teaching to ensure that the true tradition was passed down. We must remember that everything the apostles preached about Jesus and everything written in the New Testament was written about a Jesus who had risen from the dead and who they believed lived. It was their belief in the resurrection that gave an interpretation to everything that Jesus had ever done or said. In my youth I used to read a lot of Agatha Christie novels. I hardly ever managed to get more that half way through when the temptation became too great to read the last chapter to discover 'who done it'. Once I knew the end of the story my image of the characters was changed. It is because the gospel writers were writing with hindsight and because they were writing what they heard from others and editing the story for a particular public within the context of existing Christian communities, we can be certain of very little about the actual events in the life of Jesus or of his actual words.

The apostles' declaration that 'Jesus is Lord' (Acts 2:36) contained the implication that everything he had said (or was reported to have said) must be true and that all he had promised would come about.

Thirdly, organisation became necessary; overseers had to be appointed. What started simply as a sect within Judaism — 'The Way' — became an institution, an elaborate religion, so that 'Christians' became a third

187

religious group alongside Jews and Pagans, a force to be reckoned with in the Roman Empire.

With the conversion to Christianity of the Roman Emperor Constantine, in the 4th century, came the birth of Christendom, whereby the whole of the then known world was prevailed upon to live by Christian values, and the Church began to exercise temporal power. The history of our understanding of Jesus' message about the Kingdom is read in the history of the Church, and the history of the Church is read in the political history of Europe. It is said that Charlemagne saw himself as the new David and had his throne in Aachen modelled after the throne of Solomon.

A CHURCH OF POWER

Having lost sight of its purpose vis-a-vis the Kingdom, the Church exercised its presence in the world in many ways which we can now judge from our present-day understanding as being detrimental to, rather than supportive of, the values of the Kingdom. We can name three such ways in particular. First, there was the presumption that Popes and Bishops should possess a power parallel to, and in some cases even greater than, the temporal rulers in order to fulfil their spiritual office. Pope Innocent II in the 13th Century was the most powerful ruler in the whole of Europe. In 1302 Pope Boniface VIII declared himself to be the most powerful man in the world with the right to rule over kings! Between the 12th and 17th centuries most European bishops ruled over large estates and even over whole regions of a country. Of the eight 'electors' of the Emperor in Germany, four were Bishops who had this right because they were rulers of Provinces.

A second form of misuse of power, this time spiritual, was the 'force' employed to preserve the supremacy of the Christian faith — the Crusades in order to destroy the Infidel, and the Inquisition as a treatment for heretics — and always with such concern for everyone's eternal salvation! Then thirdly, from the 15th century onwards, the Church identified with the morality of the trading or middle-classes, a characteristic that is still noticeable today, whether it be its support for the 'rights' of the great land-owners or corrupt dictators in parts of Latin America or the Church's investments in pan-national corporations involved in the arms trade, or its dubious speculations on the world financial market. The Brazilian Franciscan Leonardo Boff, one of the leading protagonists for Liberation Theology, wrote in his book *The Church: Charism and Power*, using Marxist language: 'Sacred power has been the object of a process of expropriation of the means of religious production on the part of the clergy, to the detriment of the Christian people'.

The existence to this day of the Vatican as a State is an incongruous hangover from a past age, as are all the implications of a Church having as much say at the United Nations as the 193 countries making up its membership. While the Vatican's designation is a 'Non-member State Permanent Observer' it has its place on the floor of the chamber and can make an intervention at any time, just as can any other national delegation. What is the origin of this odd situation? The Papal States were lost to the Pope in 1870 in the reunification of Italy. In 1929 the government of Mussolini made compensation and granted sovereignty to the Popes in the small enclave around St Peter's Basilica. The authority of Mussolini to have done so is questionable. The 'Holy See' owes its participation in the United Nations to the earlier membership of Vatican City in the Universal Postal Union and the International Telecommunications Union which the city-state joined because of its operation of postal and radio services. Soon after its formation in 1946 the United Nations invited members of these organisations to attend its sessions on an *ad hoc* basis. The Holy See began attending the General Assembly, the World Health Organisation and UNESCO in 1951 as an observer. In 1956 the Holy See was elected a member of the UN Economic and Social Council and became a full member of the International Atomic Energy Agency! In 1964 Pope Paul VI named his permanent observer and the then Secretary General, U Thant, accepted the designation. Being treated as a State, the Vatican issues its own passports, enters into treaties on the juridical equal of any State and has its Embassies (Nunciatures) in almost every country. Leaving aside the colossal expense of this great charade, such display of temporal power is surely a complete antithesis of the Good News of Jesus: indeed, a counter-witness. Increasingly today there are movements of laity within the Catholic Church which are speaking out against this anomaly.

THE PRESENT PERIOD OF CHRISTIANITY

Karl Rahner, the well known German theologian, believed that in our century the Church, in moving out from being a western-based Church to becoming a world-wide multicultural Church, is making as great a step as it took in moving out of Palestine into the Gentile culture in its early days. This major step is one of the causes of the awakening interest today in the whole concept of

Jesus' vision of the 'Kingdom' as different from and as greater than the Church. What signs are there of this?

First, the Church is sharing in the worldwide concern for the future of humanity caused by our growing awareness that the whole of humankind is inextricably bound together in moving forward to one common destiny; an awareness that is born of the ease of immediate communication between all parts of our globe, of our increasing economic interdependence and of the insight we have received from quantum physics of the inter-relatedness of absolutely everything in nature.

Secondly, the Church finds itself growing into a new relationship with the world, the whole world, with its variety of cultures. The last one hundred and fifty years saw an unprecedented expansion of missionary activity which has brought Christianity into dialogue with other great world religions. This same expansion has exposed the counter-witness given by the apparent rivalry between different groups of Christians competing to claim Church members in the name of the same Christ. It has been said that where there is faith there is fighting!

Thirdly, the last few decades have seen the Church develop a new theology of the human person, under-standing its task as being concerned, not simply with soul matters, but with the development of the whole person and of the whole of humanity: 'What must be aimed at is complete humanisation. And what is that if not the fully rounded development of the whole person and of all people?' *(Populorum progressio* N.42 of Pope Paul VI, 1967)

Fourthly, the Church has been reflecting on its own identity. Going back to its biblical origins, it has come to a deeper understanding of its nature and its role in the world. It is this rediscovery of itself as the sign of the Kingdom that we must now explore.

A CHURCH-CENTRED THEOLOGY

Many of us passed through our Sunday School, learning the catechism, at a time when a Church-oriented theology still pertained. It was Church-oriented because the Kingdom of God was more often spoken of as the Kingdom of Heaven and this was equated with what was named the 'Church Triumphant'. The Church on Earth (the Church Militant) was militant against the powers of evil, symbolised by 'the world'. The Church was battling against a corrupt 'fallen' world from which it snatched people for their salvation.

For many centuries the Church traded on the axiom: 'Outside the Church no salvation'. Although the phrase is usually linked with St Cyprian it actually goes back to St Ignatius of Antioch in the 1st century. We must remember that St Cyprian, Bishop of Carthage, North Africa, was addressing a warning to those who had been baptised but were separating themselves from the Church wilfully: heretics and schismatics. With the spread of Christianity throughout the empire St John Chrysostom extended the meaning to include Jews and pagans under the presumption that they were equally guilty for not having become Christians! In the 13th century the axiom found its way into the official documents issued by the Church's teaching authority. A letter of Pope Innocent III in 1208 explicitly refers to there being no salvation for those outside the *Roman* Church. In 1302 Pope Boniface VIII issued a bull *Unam Sanctam* at a time when there was much discussion about the inter-relationship of the temporal power and the spiritual power. The main part of the text runs:

> That there is only one, holy, catholic and apostolic Church
> we are compelled by faith to believe and hold, and we firmly

believe in her, outside of whom there is no salvation, nor remission of sins ... Furthermore, we declare, state and define that it is absolutely necessary for the salvation of all people that they submit to the Roman Pontiff.

Even as late as 1442 we find in the text of the Council of Florence:

[The Holy Roman Church]... firmly believes, professes and preaches that 'no one remaining outside the Catholic Church, not only pagans', but also Jews, heretics and schismatics, can become partakers of eternal life; but they will go to the 'eternal fire prepared for the devil and his angels' unless before the end of their life they are joined to it.

Consequently, the Church's missionary task was to 'convert' individuals — as many as possible — and bring them into the Church. In our own times, in 1960, a Congress on World Mission in Chicago, at which were gathered representatives of many Protestant Churches, made a similar declaration:

In the days since the war more than one billion souls have passed into eternity and more than half of these went into the torment of hell fire without even hearing of Jesus Christ or why he died on the Cross of Calvary.

For this group too, evangelism means increasing Church membership as the only means of salvation. This concentration on personal salvation makes of religion a very individualistic affair, and the parish, with its various activities, is regarded as a spiritual filling station where a lot of individuals go to be 'topped up' on Sundays. The effect of this understanding of Church life causes parish life to revolve around the administration of the Sacraments, where the role of the priest is chiefly cultic and sacra-mental, and where the outreach of the parish is chiefly towards the 'lapsed', the fallen-away.

During the 1930s and 1940s a shift began to take place with a swing away from the idea of the Kingdom as an other-worldly reality to an appreciation that God was obviously active, albeit through the Church, in secular events too. This was in a period when the Church was being understood less as an institution but as the 'Mystical Body of Christ'. A phenomenon of this period was the rise of several lay movements through which the laity could share in the mission of the Church - provided their activity was strictly under clerical control! In the case of the Catholic Church it started to become involved in a number of secular activities in different countries, but always with the understanding that they were Church-controlled, which meant Hierarchy-controlled! We saw the emergence of Catholic political parties, Catholic daily newspapers and radio stations, Catholic building societies, Catholic housing associations and credit unions, Catholic Scouts and Guides. Many of these are still with us, particularly the Catholic hospitals, hospices and nursing homes and Catholic schools. The Church was emerging from the sanctuary, but only in order to 'churchify' the world's institutions.

During the 1950s and 1960s the world-Church opposition gave way to an understanding of the role of the Church within and as part of the world; indeed at the heart of the world as leaven in the dough.

The history of humanity is now appreciated as one — the world is the place of God's action, drawing all things into unity with Himself — and not as two parallel histories, the one secular and profane, the other 'salvation history' as it has been called. From being a sanctuary Church to which people fled from the world in order to find therein their salvation, it was to become again what it was originally intended to be: a sign Church, an announcement by its message and by its community life, of the Kingdom life-style that God wishes for all humanity.

> The Church is that segment of the world which reveals the final goal towards which God is working for the whole world

is a description appearing in a World Council of Churches document *(Church for Others)* which finds its parallel in documents of the Second Vatican Council of the 1960s:

> For this the Church was founded: that by spreading the Kingdom of Christ everywhere... it might bring all people to share in Christ's saving redemption (AA 2).
> It [the Church] becomes on Earth the initial budding forth of the Kingdom (LG 5).
> The Church has a single intention: that God's Kingdom may come (GS 45)

and it is the vocation of Christians to be 'artisans of a new humanity' (GS 30).

It is clear that the Church's relationship with the world is quite changed by this new understanding of its role as service to the world.

A NEW UNDERSTANDING OF MISSION

The Church is not the totality of the Kingdom but is at the service of the Kingdom. It is not correct to say that the Church alone carries on the Kingdom mission of Jesus. Say rather, the Kingdom mission of Jesus has a Church to carry it on. During the last decades there has been a change in the Church's motivation for 'mission', from evangelism — drawing people into Church membership — to evangelisation which was described, in the words of Pope Paul VI in 1975 as:

> affecting and as it were upsetting, through the power of the Gospel, mankind's criteria of judgement, determining values,

points of interest, lines of thought, sources of inspiration and models of life, which are in contrast with the Word of God and the plan of salvation *(Evangelii Nuntiandi N. 19).*

In other words, it is about challenging cultures.

The World Council of Churches' document of 1968 already quoted, describes the change in these words:

In the past it has been customary to maintain that God is related to the world through the Church. When we sharpen this view into a formula, the sequence would be: God-Church-world. This has been understood to mean that God is primarily related to the Church and only secondarily to the world by means of the Church. Further, it has been held that God relates himself to the world through the Church in order to gather everyone possible from the world into the Church. God, in other words, moves through the Church to the world. We believe that the time has come to question this sequence and to emphasise an alternative. According to this alternative the last two items in God-Church-world should be reversed, so that it reads instead God-world-Church. That is, God's primary relationship is to the world, and it is the world and not the Church that is the focus of God's plan.

This change of understanding that has been going on during the last five decades regarding the relationship of the Church to the world, occasioned by a renewed appreciation of what Jesus was saying in terms of the Kingdom, can be seen also in a parallel development, on the one hand of the reason for 'mission', and on the other, the reason for the Church's concern for social matters and how the two have drawn together. In the pre-1940s the great motivation for mission outreach (to what were then called the 'foreign missions') was to 'save souls' as individuals, while social work was undertaken because to exercise social charity was the work of a good Christian. In the 1950s the purpose of 'mission' to the Third World countries became more community-centred:

it was to establish the Church, the success of which was usually measured by the success of establishing a native clergy. Social work in this period was seen as a positive contribution to developing countries as a way of inserting Christian values. Now, in the last four decades, in an era when Liberation Theology has taken the stage in the developing world, the Church understands its concern must be equally with spiritual and material development — with the development of the whole person — because both are the concern of that Kingdom which God is bringing about beyond the Church's visible influence, and which the Church has the special task of enunciating by its spoken and lived message.

DIVISIONS AMONG CHRISTIANS

The major divisions that exist between Christians today are less the classical divides between different denominations — whether one is Methodist or Baptist or Anglican or Roman Catholic — but rather depend upon whether one is a fundamentalist or an ecumenist, a charismatic-pentecostal or a meditator, or whether one's life is Church-oriented or Kingdom-oriented. *(See the Table page 200).*

Today there are, among Christians generally, two extreme understandings of the Church-Kingdom relationship. The first, lingering from past times, is in the complete identity of the Church with the Kingdom so that there is still belief in the literal understanding of the axiom 'outside the Church there is no salvation'. The other is that Jesus never meant to found a Church but that it came into being when the apostles realised that the second coming of the Christ was not imminent. We cannot help but notice that St Paul speaks of Jesus as the 'foundation' — not the founder — of the Church (I Corinthians 3:11).

197

CHURCH ORIENTED	KINGDOM ORIENTED
Concerned with Church activities, religious behaviour, spiritual matters, because these are the concerns of the Church.	Concerned with all human behaviour, everything God has made, because these are the concerns of the Gospel.
Distinguish between the spiritual and the secular.	See human affairs are saturated with spiritual meaning and Kingdom signifiance.
Put Church membership above concern for justice and mercy.	Seek first the Kingdom of God, believing all else will follow.
Think about how to get people into the Church.	Think about how to promote the Kingdom in the world.
Outreach is to the lapsed, the fallen.	Outreach is to everyone, to effect change in society.
Concerned that the Church might be influenced by the world.	Concerned that Christians are not influencing the world.
Settle for the *status quo* and their own (respectable) kind of people.	More concerned with the poor, the widow, the orphan, the marginalised.
Ministry is centered around orthodox belief and sacramental life.	Ministry is centred around proclamation and the means to live the Gospel values.
Worship is primarily for God's glory.	Worship is primarily for people's spiritual growth.
Live very private religious lives.	Build up a community as witness to the Gospel unity of humanity.
Regard those who are baptised as the New People of God.	Regard all who promote the Kingdom values, baptised or not, whether Christian or not, as the New People of God.
Concerned with the state of body and soul — principally the latter.	Concerned with the healing and health of the whole person.
Believe that each denomination should act separately in all matters except where we are compelled to act together.	Believe that all Christians should act together in all matters except those in which deep differences of conviction compel us to act separately.

And so to our present time, an exciting time, a time of increasingly rapid change, a time of great new possibilities.

Over the millions of years during which creation has evolved — from matter to plants to animals to human beings — the evolutionary thrust has been passive, deterministic. The process has taken place without being a conscious development, without any choice being made on the part of the subjects of change. The next great step, the evolution of consciousness, by the very fact of its self-reflective nature, is of a different order. It can come about only because it is willed: because humanity, acting with freedom and deliberation, chooses to co-operate with the divine creative energy to bring about maximum consciousness, the *Omega* point.

Teilhard de Chardin wrote already in 1936:

> We now have to accept it as proven that mankind has just entered into what is probably the most extensive period of transformation it has known since its birth...Today something is happening to the whole structure of human consciousness: a fresh kind of life is beginning to appear *(The Salvation of Mankind: Thoughts on the Present Crisis)*.

He names two conditions for the *Omega* point to be reached. The first is that we be on our guard against the pessimism and despondency that might cause us to recoil from the effort required to promote this break-through. Any retreat into the negativity of our world, into a life-style which is a flight from the world's reality, or indeed any harbouring of negative thoughts about humanity's future, can only be an obstacle to the free flow of God's creative energy. The second condition, the very reverse of the first, is that we commit ourselves to positive action to promote the evolutionary process.

We have not only to believe in its possibility, but to utter with deepest conviction, that plea we make each time we say the Lord's Prayer: 'Thy Kingdom *come*, thy will be done on *Earth* as it is in Heaven...'

This conviction calls us to be more loving towards all humanity, since the *Omega* point is also the climax and crown of universal love, the fulfilment of the Kingdom. We have to summon all the energies of which we are capable to promote and foster unity and love, the great constructive forces of the future.

This requires us to understand the *Omega* point not simply as the climax of a biological process, nor even as the final goal of the human condition, but as Someone on whom our human love is focused: the Christ, in whom and through whom total unity will be achieved.

"The teachings of all the mystical paths of the world make it clear that there is within us an enormous reservoir of power, the power of wisdom and compassion, the power of what Christ called the Kingdom of Heaven" writes Sogyal Rinpoche in *The Tibetan Book of Living and Dying*.

I conclude this chapter with words of the Catholic Bishops at the Second Vatican Council, echoing Teilhard de Chardin; words from which the title of this book is drawn:

> The future of humanity lies in the hands of those who are strong enough to provide coming generations with reasons for living and hoping' (GS.31).

FIVE MAJOR STAGES OF GROWTH IN AWARENESS OF GOD'S INTENT TO UNITE THE WHOLE OF CREATION IN CHRIST

THE FIVE STAGES	PERIOD	AGENTS	JOURNEY OF GROWTH	LIMITATION	LOCATION	'THE GOD ERA'	Refs.
Foundation	Pre-history						Eph.1:4-5 Rom.1:2 GS.24
First awareness	2,000 years of early Jewish history	Jewish race 'People of God'	Many gods, their god, one God. Covenant between a tribe and God	The privileged race	Palestine	God as transient, as Almighty	LG.9
Manifestation in terms of the Kingdom of God	The Jesus event. 3 years	Jesus, the icon of God	Mission: to proclaim the Kingdom by his life and his teaching	Within Jewish culture	Palestine	God immanent, as familiar	Lk.4:43 LG.5 AG.3
Christianity	2,000 years Kingdom-Church identity	The Church 'The New People of God'	Personal salvation through Jesus	Within the Church Universal but restricted	Other —worldly		LG.1,5
Global	Third Millennium	All people of good will	Inner & Social dimension. God acts in his world. Church is 'focus' of the Kingdom	All humanity Planetary	'A New Earth'	God as Spirit	Our Father EN.23 LG.9 GS.22,39,40

PART THREE

Living the Vision Today

The Christian community 'has always had the duty of scrutinising the signs of the times and of interpreting them in the light of the Gospel'.

— The world's Catholic Bishops
at the Second Vatican Council.
1962-1965 (GS. 4)

10
A Renewed Church for Our Times

In Part One we identified and interpreted many of the characteristics of our present day that mark it out as a time of transition: a time of extremely rapid change, a time of seeming chaos and uncertainty, yet a time which is revealing the emergence of a new, deeper conscious-ness.

In Part Two we studied the vision for our world that Jesus experienced in his own life and announced in the metaphor of 'The Kingdom of God', and we saw what became of his Good News over the last two thousand years.

In this Third Part we bring the two together. We confront the characteristics of our times with the vision of Jesus in order to know what, as Christians, we should be promoting and encouraging so that they further God's overall design for humanity, and what we should be denouncing and opposing because they militate against that design.

READING THE SIGNS OF THE TIMES

The expression 'the signs of the times' is used colloquially today to refer to the special characteristics of our age.

We speak of increasing unemployment or the rise in the cost of living or the increase in violence as signs of the times. The theologial use of this phrase goes back to Jesus' own days. In Matthew's Gospel we read that

> Some Pharisees and Sadducees who came to Jesus wanted to trap him, so they asked him to perform a miracle for them, to show that God approved of him. But Jesus answered, 'When the sun is setting you say "We are going to have fine weather because the sky is red". And early in the morning you say "It is going to rain because the sky is red and dark." You can predict the weather by looking at the sky, but you cannot interpret the signs of the times!' (16:1-3).

Here it has a quite special meaning, which is that we can interpret what we experience as being the hand of God in human history. In this instance, displayed through the presence of Jesus in their midst. The bulk of Jesus' followers were the poor, the peasants of Galilee. They were the most open to his radical message because they had nothing to lose. They were powerless. Here was a man with a message of hope. In his eyes they counted for something, they were valued by the God he kept referring to as his and their Father. They had all to gain by accepting the new way of life that he not only proposed to them but proved was realistic by living that way himself. Those who were most threatened by his message were those with power. They felt their authority was being challenged. To accept him would spell their ruin. Their very status in society was being undermined by this preacher. Such were the Pharisees and Sadducees. The role of the Pharisees, a sect in Jewish society, was to further the knowledge and practice of the Law of Moses and to apply it to the circumstances of their own day. The Sadducees were a priestly party who controlled the Temple and Jewish worship. They belonged to the aristocratic upper level of society and were conservative in their views.

To the minds of both groups this revolutionary Galilean prophet had to be exposed as a charlatan. And yet there must have been an element of truth in his words which resonated deeply within them. They needed to be quite sure of themselves before exposing him. They would surely have witnessed some of his miracles, all of which were 'signs' to those with open minds. The report of the first miracle in John's gospel about the turning of water into wine at the wedding of friends, ends with the words: 'Jesus performed this first *sign* in Cana of Galilee' (2:11). The healing of the nobleman's son is called 'the second *sign* (4:54) and at the end of this gospel we read: 'Jesus did many other *signs* which are not written in this book' (20:30). Luke, reporting on Jesus' triumphal entry into Jerusalem amid the palm-waving crowds, at the close of his ministry, says that the large crowd praised him 'for all the *signs* that they had seen' (19:37).

What the Pharisees and Sadducees required was some physical sign that could leave them in no possible doubt. From the reply Jesus gave we might guess they asked for a sign in the sky. Maybe the sort of sign that the prophet Joel had foretold:

> I will give warnings on that day in the sky and on the Earth; there will be bloodshed, fire and clouds of smoke. The Sun will be darkened and the Moon will turn as red as blood before the great and terrible day of the Lord comes. (Joel 2:30-31).

But Jesus never exerted that kind of psychological pressure on anyone to accept his message. To have done so would have removed their freedom of choice in accepting him as the promised Messiah. His reply was that signs abound for those whose hearts are open enough to notice and interpret them: to interpret the signs of God's action in their midst.

So we notice two elements here: the sign itself and the interpretation of that sign. A sign is a symbol. It points to something beyond itself. Unless it is interpreted it has no significance as a sign. The first time I visited the small African country of Malawi, in the 1960s, there was only one set of traffic lights in the whole country, and that was to regulate traffic crossing a very narrow bridge in the centre of one of the towns. For the peasants coming into town from the rural villages these pillars of changing lights were a facination and things of beauty. But no more than that. They were signs only to those who could interpret the message conveyed by the changing colours.

We have to move beyond the sign to that which it signifies. Gregory Bateson, the anthropologist, wrote of the difference between knowing a country by studying a map (the sign) and actually experiencing the countryside (the reality). He said that to stop at the sign is like coming to a restaurant and eating the menu instead of the meal!

In the whole history of God's relationship with humanity, as related in the Hebrew Scriptures and the Christian New Testament, people have understood God to communicate Himself through actions. These actions are signs. They require interpretation before they become a meaningful communication, what, in theological language, is called God's Revelation.

Within our Jewish-Christian tradition we can trace the path of humanity's growth in its knowledge of God through the process of, first the Jews and later the Christians, reflecting upon God's actions in relation to themselves and then, with the aid of enlightenment by the Spirit, interpreting what they experienced as signs of God's presence with his people and of the direction in which He was leading them.

The first of the historical events in this process to be recorded was the call of the patriarch Abraham to go to a new country and begin to form God's special tribe.

The interpretation of these events occurred only very much later. It was while the new tribe of Israelites was wandering in the desert, having been liberated against all odds from their slavery to the Pharaohs in Egypt, that they reflected upon these events and interpreted them as signs of God's powerful presence among them, and came to the conclusion that step by step they were being led by God to a special destiny. They were reading 'the signs of the times': the signs of what they understood to be God's frequent saving intervention in their history.

Right up to the end of Jesus' life on Earth the small group of his disciples had still not understood the significance of who he was or the purpose of his mission. Luke reports that just before his Ascension they asked Jesus: 'Lord will you at this time give the Kingdom back to Israel?' (Acts 1:6). It was only after their enlightenment by the Spirit at Pentecost that the young community of Jesus' followers was able to reflect on the Jesus-event and interpret the significance for the whole of humanity of the life, death and resurrection of Jesus; of what Jesus had really meant by the Kingdom.

It is therefore life as we experience it today that we must examine to detect whether it manifests signs that we are, or are not, heading in the direction of God's design for humanity: the Kingdom of God. This is what we mean by a theological reading of the signs of the times. 'Theological', because we are not reading the events and trends of our times as would an economist or a politician, but with the eyes of faith, confronting the signs with God's communication of Himself as interpreted in the pages of Scripture, in order to read them in a God perspective.

This is not only a continual task for each one of us but is the task of the Christian community as a whole: the continuing task of the Church.

I have mentioned trends. By trends I mean those phenomena which are not one-off events, however significant, but ideas or movements within society which we see gaining popularity. They are the particular tides which appear to be sweeping us forwards in a certain direction, whether creatively or destructively.

It would fill volumes to assess the Kingdom value of every phenomenon we identified in Part One. On the next page, however, I have listed some of the trends that are often regarded as characteristic of our new age. I suggest that these fall under what we might call three Key Trends. Namely:

— a new era of awareness

— a search for unity

— a re-awakening of the spiritual dimension of life.

We can be helped to make a Christian evaluation of these by taking note of words attributed to Jesus and to passages in the New Testament which relate to these three Key Trends, if not to all the phenomena listed beneath them.

A *new era of awareness.* During his Last Supper with his intimate friends around him Jesus said:

> I have much more to tell you but now it would be too much for you to bear. When, however, the Spirit comes, who reveals the truth about God, he will lead you into all the truth. He will not speak on his own authority, but he will speak of what he hears, and will tell you of things to come. He will give me glory, because he will take what I say and tell it to you (John 16:12-14).

So while traditionally it is said that there is to be no further new revelation since Jesus' day, there will continue to be an increasing awareness of the depth of meaning in what he told us.

210

A Few Manifestations of the Three Key Trends

A New Era of Awareness

Quantum physics: everything inter-related
Eastern forms of meditation
The Gaia hypothesis: Earth a living organism
Resurgence of feminine values
Left/right brain harmony
Appreciation of Vedic Science
Desire of the young for authenticity
Discovery of Ley Lines
Concern for justice and human rights
New cosmology. Astrophysics
Adult creativity. 'University of the Third Age'
Appreciation of indigenous cultures (African, Aborigines, Native American)
The information explosion
Experience of pluralistic, multi-ethnic societies
Collapse of long-standing ideological barriers
From colonial domination to independent nations
The questioning of authority

A Search for Unity

PERSONAL

Personal growth workshops
Health Farms
Body, mind, spirit harmony
Organic food. Vegetarianism
Healing rather than curing
Yoga classes
Complementary medicine
Urge to reconnect with the body: emotions, feelings, intuition

RELATIONAL

Valuing participation, democracy
The community movement
'One World Week'
Ecumenism. Inter-Faith dialogue
Response to disaster appeals
Growing together: UN, EC, OAU
Globalisation

COSMIC

Ecology and Green issues
The Green Party
Organic farming
Creation spirituality
'Deep Ecology'
Animal rights

A Re-awakening of the Spiritual dimension of Life

A change in our perception of God
Increasing belief in reincarnation
Tarot cards
Channelling
The Hospice movement
Devas/Angels
Desire for spiritual experience
Astrology
Emergence of new sects
Move from formal religion to spirituality
Uniformity giving way to unity in diversity
Resurgence of Goddess spirituality
Interest in esoteric disciplines
Search for the mystical
Appreciation of Eastern spirituality
Return to Celtic spirituality

211

Mark relates that when Jesus first went public with his Good News he announced:

> 'The right time has come', he said, 'and the Kingdom of God is at hand. Turn from your evil ways and believe the Good News!' (Mark 1:15).

We have already seen how the Greek word *metanoia* translated here as 'turn away from your evil ways' is more accurately translated as 'put on a new mind', 'have a new mind set', 'expand your consciousness' or 'deepen your awareness'. Only thus are we going to be able to recognise the presence of the Kingdom around us.

A search for unity. John's gospel recounts how during his long address and shared prayer with his dearest friends at his Last Supper, Jesus prayed above all for unity. Having prayed for those around him he went on to pray for all those who would hear his Good News through them:

> I pray not only for them, but also for those who believe in me because of their message. I pray that they may all be one, Father! May they be in us, just as you are in me and I am in you. May they be one, so that the world will believe that you sent me. I gave them the same glory you gave me, so that they may be one, just as you and I are one. I in them and you in me, so that they may be completely one, in order that the world may know that you sent me and that you love them as you love me (John 17:20-23).

There could hardly be a more expressive way of pleading for human unity, a unity of the quality of Jesus' own experience of the highest form of unity, what we call 'unity consciousness'. And he prays not only that his disciples will experience the same but that through the way they live their unity all the world might come to know that heart of the Kingdom message that he believed God had sent him to proclaim.

212

We have already met that passage from the Letter to the Ephesians in which is summed up, perhaps more clearly than in any other place in the New Testament, God's design for humanity: everything and everyone united in the Christ:

> In all his wisdom and insight God did what He had purposed, and made known to us the secret plan He had already decided to complete by means of the Christ. This plan, which God will complete when the time is right, is to bring all creation together, everything in the heavens and on Earth, with the Christ as head (Ephesians 1:8-11).

A re-awakening of the spiritual dimension of life. Once again the scene is the Last Supper:

> I am telling you the truth: whoever believes in me will do what I do — yes, he will do even greater things, because I am going to the Father (John 14:12).

We said previously that the 'signs' or miracles that Jesus performed were possible because he was so God-filled, so highly evolved as a human being, living in such a high plain of consciousness, that he was able to draw on cosmic powers. What he did, in other words, was not beyond human capacity. Here he is promising that as humanity evolves to higher planes, becomes more spiritual, we too will be able to exercise the powers he exercised — and more!

And finally, back to the Letter to the Ephesians, where the author speaks of our future as we become more Christ-filled:

> And so we shall all come together to that oneness in our faith and in our knowledge of the son of God; we shall become mature people, reaching to the very height of the Christ's full stature (4:13).

Most people today meet Christianity through the channel of the Church. The Church gives a visible, human image of what Christianity is all about and hidden beneath this image is the original Good News of Jesus. I say 'hidden' but so often it is obscured. The original vision of Jesus for an elevated humanity has been highjacked by a religious system so that the Good News has become one religion among, or rather against, others. The Kingdom vision of Jesus is a prescription for all of humanity to enable everyone to enter the next period of our transformation, our next evolutionary step, understanding 'evolution' as the progressive self-manifestation of the Divine in material creation.

His Good News was not for the select few, the 'saved'. The Church is not simply a waggon for people to clamber aboard in order to be taken to 'the other side'. There is nothing that the baptised can claim is uniquely for them. There is nothing unique about the Christian ethic which is not applicable to the whole of humanity when humankind lives its highest calling, lives at its most sublime. The Church is, and always will be, a minority community, a leaven, called to witness a Kingdom-style of living and in this way contribute to the Kingdom of God becoming a this-world reality.

The challenges posed by the Kingdom values to our present-day Church might be listed under four headings.

1. *To recognise and encourage the holistic right-brain values.*

— To encourage creativity in liturgy and worship. For example, to accept that in today's world where the majority of Christians now live in the Southern Hemisphere, different peoples need to create their own cultural expressions in worship.

— Respect must be paid to the value of spiritual experience.

This requires letting go of the fear that thereby control over Christian belief might be endangered. Left-brain thinking has been given priority over experience. Yet no one can come to God until they have had an experience of God in some way or other.

— Acknowledge the value of women's participation in the administration and ministry of the Church.

— Recover the Early Church's ministry of healing. Make spiritual healing techniques more widely known and used.

— 'In the design of God, every man is called upon to develop and fulfil himself, for every life is a vocation. This self-fulfilment is not something optional. Human fulfilment constitutes, as it were, a summary of our duties'*(Populorum Progressio* N.15,16 of Pope Paul VI*)*

2. *To accept the ecological dimension of spirituality.*

— Be unafraid of presenting the mythic nature of the creation story.

— Take on board the "new cosmology": what science (astronomy in particular) tells us about our place in the Universe. That we human beings are not the be-all and end-all of creation.

— The need to preach our partnership with, not domination of, all creatures on Earth.

3. *To be open to the necessity or continually re-assessing and then changing Church structures so that they are life-supporting, not life-draining.*

— Be a model to society of community structure as against pyramidical structure.

— Abolish grandiose clerical titles and benefices.

— Acknowledge and encourage the shift away from clericalism and a clerical caste. Bernard Häring (1912-1998) the prophetic Redemptorist priest and well-known moral theologian, spoke frankly to The National Catholic Reporter in USA in 1997 about the need of conversion and structural change in the papal office:

> Since Constantine...the Church has gradually taken on monarchical — even at times absolutist — structures, worldly trappings, triumphalistic pomp and ridiculous titles of honour...The Church that so convincingly calls

for conversion of the individual must recognise that she herself needs an in-depth renovation of structures, forms of address and mindsets, in a word, an authentic conversion.

— Develop 'Small Basic Communities' as the new local Church structure replacing the large parish as the locus for Christians to meet. That such communities are increasing in popularity world-wide, in all cultures, is surely a sign of the Spirit inspiring this way forward.

— Be open to new forms of professed Religious life, new forms of community living, as giving a more appropriate witness of the Kingdom.

— The 'preferential option for the poor' means being more positive in welcoming into the community the minorities, the alienated, those on the fringe of society.

— Admit past errors and that past moral and doctrinal statements are not set in stone but are always in need of re-expression.

— Every Christian Church must give up its fundamentalist cast of mind: that it alone possesses the fullness of truth. Such an attitude is religious tribalism which is poles apart from that required for a planetary civilisation, the vision of the Kingdom. Recently, Bishop Pierre Claverie of Oran, Algeria, wrote: 'It is my conviction that humanity can only exist in the plural. As soon as we [Catholics] claim to possess the truth or speak in the name of humanity we fall into totalitarianism and exclusion. No one possesses the truth; everyone seeks it'.

4. *To be open to the Spirit.*

— 'It is the world that must be allowed to provide the agenda for the Churches. The Church exists for the world' *(WCC document The Church for Others. 1968)*. This does not mean the Church should follow current fashion but that there is a constant reading of 'the signs of the times' to discern signs of the Spirit's action within humanity.

— Encourage individuals to follow their consciences in their spiritual search, allowing that sometimes this may take them outside the Church. 'The Truth cannot impose itself except by virtue of its own truth' (DH.1).

— Liberate people from what Jesus wished to liberate us from:

216

— the dead-weight of doctrine. God requires our growth in love, not in knowledge. Knowledge is only a means to that end.

— the burden of guilt and of divine retribution laid upon people by bad religious education.

— the need for an intermediary between ourselves and God, whether it be Jesus*, Mary or the priest-hood. 'In union with the Christ and through our faith in him we have the boldness to go into God's presence with all confidence' (Ephesians 3:12).

— whatever prevents us recognising the presence of the Divine in everyone and everything.

— any inhibition about expressing doubts in belief.

— Be less absolutist. Respect the difference between values and those techniques which promote them. For example, Church-attendance is a 'technique' to foster spiritual growth, not an end in itself. Be constantly alert to the danger of making absolute what is relative. 'The Sabbath was made for people, and not people for the Sabbath' (Mark 2:27)

— Promote dialogue between different Faiths, not on a basis of superiority but as equals searching for Truth

— Accept to be challenged by the changing values in society. To be open to them rather than defensive.

---

* *The gospel of John has Jesus say: 'I am the way, the truth and the life; no one comes to the Father except by me' (14:6). There are other words of Jesus reported by John which seem to support Jesus' role as unique mediator between humanity and his Father, for instance: 'I am the gate for the sheep...whoever comes in by me will be saved', (10:7-9). Many contemporary theologians (eg. Maurice Wiles, John B.Cobb, K. Rahner, R.Panikkar) affirm that the Logos of Christ, eternal and universal, has been incarnated in Jesus of Nazareth. All such quotations are from the Gospel of John which applies them to the Christ, the Logos, the Divine Word, 'and are wrongly taken to refer exclusively to a particular human being', Jesus of Nazareth. 'Like other statements in the same gospel (such as "before Abraham was, I am") they are to be understood as referring to the Logos rather than to Jesus the first-century historical figure' (Maurice Wiles).*

— Give priority to love-in-action over adherence to a set of beliefs as criteria for Church membership. A Church in which people are unkind to each other or suppress each other is not a true Church. The Holy Spirit is not there.

— Teach and encourage the practice of deep meditation, (borrowing centuries-old techniques coming from the East) as one of the principal means of spiritual growth. 'No movement in religious life has any value unless it is also a movement inwards to the "still centre" of your existence, where Christ is' (Pope John Paul II, in Ireland. 1979).

I conclude this chapter with a quotation from Bede Griffiths:

The organisation of the Church, with its doctrine of Trinity and Incarnation and its eucharistic ritual, has no other purpose than to communicate love, to create a community of love, to unite all people in the eternal Ground of being, which is present in the heart of everyone. This is the criterion by which the Church is to be judged, not by the forms of its doctrine or ritual, but by the reality of the love which it manifests. *(Return to the Centre.)*

Bishop John Spong in his book *Resurrection: Myth or Reality?* gives the same message more succinctly: 'The business of the Church is to love people into life'.

Re-visioning the Church

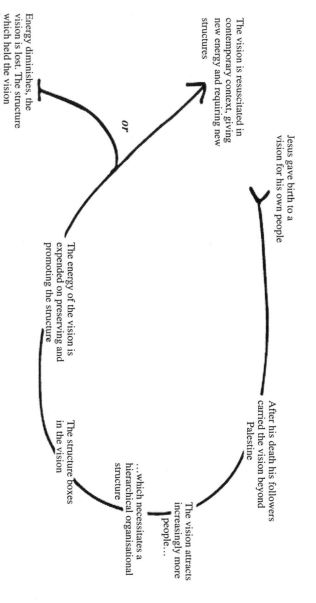

Jesus gave birth to a vision for his own people

After his death his followers carried the vision beyond Palestine

The vision attracts increasingly more people...

...which necessitates a hierarchical organisational structure

The structure boxes in the vision

The energy of the vision is expended on preserving and promoting the structure

Energy diminishes, the vision is lost. The structure which held the vision becomes irrelevant

or

The vision is resuscitated in contemporary context, giving new energy and requiring new structures

11

Artisans of a New Humanity

The Christian's vocation is a call to participate in making the Reign of God a reality. It is an invitation to be an 'artisan of a new humanity'. The contribution of each of us is unique. It is to co-operate with God's Spirit to transform our world at this moment of its history. This requires of us that we make four paradigm shifts in our relationships. Namely, our relationship to our Planet Earth, our relationship with each other as human inhabitants of our one world, our relationship with God as an expression of the Ultimate Reality that cannot be expressed, and finally with ourselves: the relationship between our false self and the person God dreams of our becoming.

A NEW RELATIONSHIP TO PLANET EARTH

Advances in knowledge in three areas of human life demand that we re-adjust our perspective. The first concerns advances made in science and technology. These are being applied to nearly every aspect of human existence. So great are the changes they are bringing about, it is as if we are living in a foreign country to that

221

of our birth. It is a 'country' in which an IBM computer can beat a Grand Master in chess in just nineteen moves, in which dead people can be frozen until a cure can be found for their illness, in which animals can be cloned from a single strand of DNA, in which a sixty-four year old mother can give birth through in-vitro fertilisation, a world from which ashes of the deceased can be rocketted into outer space to be scattered.

The second area is caused by the discoveries of astrophysicists. Astronomers are observing the explosion of distant stars in far galaxies, explosions which happened ten billion years ago, six billion years before our planet even existed. Far from thinking of ourselves as the final and most perfect product of the Creator's hand we now have to see ourselves as mere dots on a vast canvas. We all live on one rather small planet. And it was as a human being on our tiny planet that Jesus appeared and shared his vision. His vision was about our human future here, not about other possible forms of life on other galaxies and their future, nor indeed about the destiny of the Universe as a whole.

The third area of human life demanding an adjustment of our perspective is from understanding ourselves to be outside, apart from the natural world, ruling over it (shallow ecology) to realising that because every part of creation is inter-dependent, no part, including us humans, is superior to any other part (deep ecology). Having been brought up to believe that we alone are 'made in the image of God' we must come to appreciate that every creature on the planet from elephants to ants reflects the Divine in their own perfect way. We are all in need of each other.

The late Donald Nicholl, one-time rector of Tantur Ecumenical Centre in Jerusalem, wrote in *The Tablet* (2/4/88):

I believe that many of the discussions and controversies on religious issues these days are frustrating and paralyse our capacity for spiritual growth because most of us are operating with a world view at the back of our minds which is the world view of late nineteenth-century scientific materialism...a world view that made the Universe seem hostile to us and thereby made us feel ourselves to be excrescences upon it, aliens in the Universe.

A NEW RELATIONSHIP WITH EACH OTHER

To move to a new social paradigm from one that has been with us for at least six thousand years is a shift indeed! Jesus tried to introduce such a shift two thousand years ago but was singularly unsuccessful. Worse, his followers soon organised themselves on the pattern of the day and have been sustaining the hierarchy structure in the Church ever since.

However, with the increasing value being given to networking, with the world-wide call for democracy, with more and more of those who are said to be 'at the bottom of the pile' demanding a say in the future direction of their lives and the lives of their children, cracks are appearing in the pyramidal shape of power and control management. More people are seeking to regain control of their way to healthier lives, of their working pattern, of their environment, of the way their children are educated and of their cultural life. In 2000 it was estimated that 1,700 people in Britain left the cities each week to live in the countryside.

People with this new vision see the falsehood of some of the presumptions upon which our society is built, all stemming from a hierarchical paradigm. For instance, that the larger an organisation is, the more power it has, the more successful it will be; that the male should be the chief bread-winner in the family; that the principal purpose of education is to open the way to a full-time paid job, preferably with a managerial position; that it is an inevitable historical fact that the Northern Hemisphere should be more prosperous than the Southern; that God is male.

Our own contribution to this shift is made when we become aware of who is manipulating us and why, and by convincing ourselves that no one can have any power over us unless we allow them to exercise it. This is equally true when a gun is being pointed at our head as when religious leaders tell us with such conviction that their's is the only true path to salvation and what a terrible next-world fate awaits us if we do not embrace it.

Again, we contribute to the shift when we convince ourselves that former patterns of relationships — in marriage, in family life, in sexual orientation — are not set in concrete for all times but like all else in an evolving world, can be the subject of change and re-assessment. The ultimate criterion of their value being: will this new direction make us more loving, more whole people, living in greater harmony within ourselves and with others?

In his speech opening the Catholic world's Second Vatican Council in 1962 Pope John XXIII said:

> In the present order of things, Divine Providence is leading us to a new order of human relations which, by our own efforts and even beyond our very expectations, are directed towards the fulfilment of God's superior and inscrutable designs.

A NEW RELATIONSHIP TO GOD

Within his Kingdom vision Jesus introduced his hearers to a new intimacy with Divine Being, the Transcendent. Our English language reveals how different our perception of God is from that of Jesus. In our Anglo-

Saxon, Germanic languages the name we give to the Ultimate Reality, 'God', is derived from the same root as 'good': good as opposed to bad, which already reveals the dualism in our thinking. We think in terms of opposites: we oppose sacred to profane, spiritual to material, holy to irreligious, good to evil. However, the languages of the Middle East use titles from a different root. In Canaanite *Elat*, in Hebrew *Elohim*, in Arabic *Allah* and in Jesus' own language, Aramaic *Alaha*. The root of these names means *The All, Divine Unity,* the *Being of the Universe*. It was with this experience of unity that Jesus called God his Father. Although the Divine is beyond naming, we do need a handle, however inadequate, if we are to have a relationship with the Transcendent. So 'God' will have to serve us, as a shorthand, knowing how little of the reality it expresses. Similarly, the title 'Father' has its linguistic and cultural limitations. Jesus had an inexpressible experience of unity with God — 'The Father and I are one' — and the best way he found to express that was as being in a father-son relationship. But that may not be the most helpful for us. It is not the last word about God. There is no last word about God. Indeed, to insist upon just one human expression of God is a form of idolatry. Regarding God only as a father can hold us in a parent-child relationship which in a subtle way can impede our growth to maturity as adults. Increasingly more Christians today who still prefer to personify God, think of Him as a friend, a partner in life who invites us to be co-creators of our world.

Throughout the centuries of western religious history there has been an evolution in our levels of intimacy with God. In what Christians name the Old Testament era there was a creature-to-Creator relationship. God was present to the Hebrew people not in a one-to-one relationship but as a tribe in covenant with a tribal-God. Then Jesus appeared among us introducing God as a Father-God and for the two thousand years since, his followers have had this personal child-parent relationship with the source of all Being. Today, with our greater consciousness of the Spirit empowering us from within, many Christians are developing an interior relationship, partnering a God who is neither male nor female, in sustaining and bettering our planet. The God who dwells within us is much more enriching than the distant Sky God.

It is with this shift in our relationship with the Divine that problems with Christianity arise for so many people, both within and outside the Church. In all fields of human concern — psychology, sociology, politics, science, culture, ethics — we no longer express ourselves nor understand our world as our parents did. Yet the language of the Church — whether expressed in theological explanations, in symbols of worship or in the wording of hymns — has seen no change since medieval times. It is still talking a language we no longer speak. Little wonder the Church and its message seem to so many to bear no relationship to life as experienced today. The Church is in a box apart.

Again, in that same opening speech Pope John XXIII said: 'The substance of the ancient doctrine of the deposit of faith is one thing, and the way it is presented is another'. All our doctrinal statements are partial expressions of mysteries the totality of which is beyond our comprehension. Hence no such expression has an eternal value. To be true to the mystery we need to attempt to re-express it in accordance with the knowledge and thinking of our own times. To attempt to do so is not a disloyalty to 'revelation': on the contrary, to preserve these expressions in a form that no longer has meaning for today would be the disloyalty, depriving them of their power to nourish us spiritually. Which is not to say previous expressions of belief were erroneous. They were composed for a people of a particular culture at a particular time in history and served them well. But they are no longer adequate for our own times. If our beliefs are to be nourishment for and enliven our way of living, they must relate to reality as we personally experience and interpret it today.

In discussions about euthanasia or about the advances of science, for example, the experimenting with genetically modified food, the cloning of living creatures and all our human attempts to control the laws of nature, indeed to bend them to our benefit, we so often hear warnings expressed as 'we are playing God' as if there were a department of life that God allows us to play with but that there are frontiers beyond which is God's area of control. And who is to say where that frontier lies? Such naive remarks assume a God who would rather we were not co-creators, despite His having given us the mental abilities so to act. (In calling ourselves co-creators with God we are not meaning that we are equal partners. Within God's continual act of creating the Universe, our field of action is only Planet Earth. In the dimension of time-space our co-operation is in giving form to or materialising God's creative energy.)

Have we not already taken a giant step over that frontier when on 6th August 1945 we wrested control from God of the very existence of our planet? It was the day we dropped the first atomic bomb, when war-making shifted from genocide to omnicide. By allowing the planet to continue to exist, despite the nuclear arsenal humanity still holds which could destroy it several times over, we have seized from 'the Almighty' the mastery over life on

Earth. But, further, with our adventures into the field of genetic engineering we have given ourselves the power to re-shape all life forms. We have really taken 'creation' into our own hands! It makes all our former attempts at 'playing God' look puny!

A NEW RELATIONSHIP WITH OURSELVES

The adjustment of this fourth relationship required of us is the most difficult of all because it depends on a shift in consciousness and this depends upon no one but ourselves.

We need to recall how Jesus gave us a condition for becoming a Kingdom person, a conversion so radical that it requires a change of mind-set, a change of consciousness (*metanoia*). We remember how he described to Nicodemus the need to be born again. This is the condition even for 'seeing' the Kingdom — as being able to recognise its coming about in our own times — let alone of 'entering' into its values. A paradigm shift, indeed!

Our mind-set has been formed throughout our life by so many influences — our family upbringing, our formal education, our ethnic culture, our genes, our experiences — that to put on 'a new mind' requires a fundamental re-think of all our attitudes, our relationships, our values and our world-vision.

There are two paths in particular that we can take to help us to make this conversion. The first is to adopt a complete openness to what we see and hear. Judgements we must make, but not with prejudice. Only the open-minded are truly able to read the 'signs of the times', because the Spirit blows where She wills, and in some surprising directions. Being open means being continually a searcher. A searcher with an open mind finds that the right person, the right word, the right experience, the right book enters our life at just the moment needed for us to learn the next lesson, to take the next step. 'When the pupil is ready, the teacher appears'. If we are not open and observant, that moment will be lost, maybe never to be repeated.

The other path is through recognising that we are all called to be mystics. 'Mysticism' is not a word in our every-day vocabulary. We associate it with a few chosen saints who reach the higher stages of spiritual experience. But mysticism is associated with mystery. It means to see beyond the material reality: to see the presence of the Divine in everything and everyone around. To be able to recognise that in the diversity of humanity — cultures, traditions, religions — lies the creativity of God. But especially it means to recognise the Divine within ourselves. The 10th century St Symeon the New Theologian (as he is called) wrote: "The greatest misfortune that can befall you as a Christian is not to know consciously that God lives within you". To be a mystic means to live from the heart, to be centred, to be whole. Everyone of us is called to be a mystic.

The practical means to take on our path towards mysticism is through a perseverance with some twice-daily form of deep meditation. We are so achievement-oriented in the West that we easily give up such a practice if we do not feel it is doing us some good. If we are to spend time on it, we want results! We forget that meditating is more than simple prayer: a spiritual exercise. It is a holistic exercise that gives nourishment and balance to body and mind as well as to spirit. Effects there certainly are but they are often very subtle and for that reason they are observable only in the long run. How the practice changes us is more often noticed by family and friends than by ourselves. Then, even less easy to quantify, but no less real, is the effect that numbers of people meditating have on their surroundings in reducing the level of stress with all the consequences of that. A truly Kingdom-promoting activity!

Can such attention to our own development, to become more the persons we are meant to be, really make the world a better place? What can one individual — even a group of individuals — hope to achieve? Let us not forget the 10% it takes to form the critical mass needed to initiate change in public consciousness. The ecologist Rudolph Bahro wrote: 'When the forms of an old culture are dying, the new culture is created by a few people who are not afraid to be insecure'.

In the Middle Ages the assumption was that the world could not be transformed. Your only hope was to leave it and go to Heaven. Then came the Renaissance with its burst of creativity followed by the Industrial Revolution which gave us the physical tools to change our environment. Today we have a further power, the development of our consciousness. This is the key to bringing about Heaven on Earth, making the vision of Jesus a reality, our next evolutionary step. And it begins with each one of us.

Let us listen to the advice of a Tibetan Buddhist, Sogyal Rinpoche: "The danger we are all in together makes it essential now that we no longer think of spiritual development as a luxury, but as a necessity for survival" (*The Tibetan Book of Living and Dying*).

'To be human is to change.
To be perfect is to have changed often.'
— *John Henry Newman*

12

To Be Human Is to Change: Our Personal Journey

From my acquaintance with Christians who are discovering the New Era of Consciousness and beginning to assess their beliefs in a new perspective, it appears to me that there are three stages through which such people seem to journey. They are:

> A period of awakening and wider vision;
> A period of challenge and exploration;
> A period of acceptance and peace.

In identifying the characteristics of each period, I am trying to record and give a sense of meaning to people's experiences as they have been recounted to me.

A PERIOD OF AWAKENING AND WIDER VISION

It starts with an intuition, however vague at first, which grows into a conviction, that some big change is coming about in our world. Much more embracing than any single event one hears about. It is a growing awareness that is supported by becoming more conscious of the meaning behind a whole range of events and observations, all of which seem to point in one direction. They were noticed before, but not as indicating this change. Now they take on a meaning; they have the same meaning.

With this new awareness of indications that some big change is coming, is a parallel awareness that you are part of it. You too are changing in some way.

The coming change implies a departure from present roots, props, securities. Especially from the unchanging anchor-hold of the Church. There is a growing sense that Church teaching, and even Church life, does not ring true with your experience.

You begin to feel that the Church is not related to life as it is lived today. There is an unreality about it. Church life seems to happen at a surface-level and not draw its life from an inner depth. Its moral teaching and its presentation of doctrine are too facile, too cut and dried, taking the human elements too little into consideration. Its teaching seems to be too rational, too left-brain, and not flow from an inner Truth.

Whereas before you were content with believing in truths about God, you now begin to experience God as Truth. This causes you to have to face the question: Can I go on relying solely on the Church as my source of Truth?

As this awareness develops it leads to a dark period of inner turmoil. The secure foundations are wobbling. A crisis looms ahead. Do you remain true to your growing inner conviction that Truth is experienced in the depth of your consciousness, or do you remain loyal to the expressions of doctrine which no longer ring true for you?

You are faced with an inability to move back to the set pattern of your old position: at the same time you do not have the courage to untie the mooring, and launch into an uncharted sea.

With this crisis your regular practice of church-going and church-involvement begins to change. This can lead to a sense of guilt at unfaithfulness. You are not helped by church-going relatives and friends who are quite uncomprehending and speak of your 'lapsing' and 'losing your faith'.

This period continues until there comes the day that you have the courage to be true to yourself and step aside from — not necessarily out of — the institutional Church. (Later, in the third period, you may step in again as a renewed person.)

What seems to be a common vehicle carrying people along this road of deepening awareness is the regular practice of some form of deep meditation or silent reflection or mindfulness: some exercise that turns you from a Sky God up there or out there, to discover the God in your own still centre.

A PERIOD OF CHALLENGE AND EXPLORATION

With increasing courage to let go, there comes the desire to venture out, to explore other avenues, other movements, other religions, other ideologies. You become a seeker. You take the risk of involvement by reading their literature, attending their meetings, making friends with their followers.

This period of searching is a lonely one. You feel estranged from family and friends — from your partner even — who think you are weird. They treat you with compassion as a lost sheep, if they do not actually set about trying to re-convert you.

This is a time when you desperately look around for a counsellor, a confidant; someone sympathetic with your search, with whom you can share your thoughts and sound out your new discoveries. This must be someone on the same wave-length who will not try to direct you but rather draw you out so that you articulate what is in your unconscious mind, thus helping you to reach a free decision. You may think of clergy or Religious within the Church as the sort of people who offer guidance on the spiritual path, but sadly it is difficult to find such a guide among them. In fact you are instinctively dissuaded from asking because you suspect the incomprehension with which your tale will be met.

And yet, as you journey, assurance and guidance come from other quarters. You notice gradually that at each step, just when the need is greatest, some person or some book or some other form of inspiration suddenly enters your life — and often from a most unexpected source. It gives you an assurance that, after all, the Holy Spirit is there as guide along the path. An assurance for the future builds up: that when guidance is needed, guidance will be there.

Related to this is a growing sense of connectedness. You become increasingly aware that there is some common thread running through all the new contacts and experiences that come your way. That somehow they are all contributing to some great movement, although that movement cannot be labelled, except to say it is the New Consciousness of which you feel you are becoming a part.

As this stage of exploration and new challenges proceeds, you move away from a desire to try to explain or defend your journey to uncomprehending friends and family and with a growing sense of relief that you are not a renegade but are being true to yourself, you become increasingly reluctant to spend your energy on trying to convince others of your new discoveries. Instead, you seek the company of like-minded people and feel a great strength in communicating with them, albeit that this communication may be silent communication as experienced in a group meditation.

DEAD ENDS

Not all people entering the first or even the second period go further. For one reason or another they are not able to take the courageous step required; not able to let go of those safe supports they have depended upon till now.

But then the whole of life, from self-centred babyhood, is a journey of letting go, right up to the ultimate act of surrendering ourselves to the Other in the naked passage of death. Each one of us makes that journey at a different pace. Not to go forward, however, is to enter a dead end. To cease to grow is to diminish.

A PERIOD OF ACCEPTANCE AND PEACE

The journey has been a journey inwards, to your 'still centre', to the depth of your consciousness. But this is not an ego-trip. It is at the same time a journey into the centre of all being, into the centre of the source of all being, all life, all love, into the wholeness, holiness, of God. There you discover the world and all creation and all people anew.

You experience a unity of all life. You find that you are relating to all creation and especially to other people in a new way. The divine life within you recognises its unity with the divine life in others to the extent that you feel that they and yourself are part of a whole.

This causes a growth in compassion: a concern for the suffering, the needy, for ecology, for mending and healing and making whole. It brings about a desire to break down the barriers that people erect to keep themselves apart, disintegrated. You promote peace. Your sense of justice is sharpened. You recognise the good in all things: the good even in the official enemies.

You appreciate the good and the truth and the sanctity found in other religions. You recognise that they are all paths, blessed by God, to lead people to the Ultimate Truth. You intuitively feel that the different religions are simply parts of a whole, a total ascent of humankind to God, and that one day the differences between them will become insignificant compared with the unity of consciousness that already unites humanity.

Your search for Truth is replacing your former reliance on truths. The different and imperfect expressions of truths diminish in importance. You gradually rely more upon the truth of your own experience. An inner authority stemming from the truth of experience gradually replaces the need to surrender to an outer authority.

With the growing acceptance that your path, though often far from clear, is absolutely right and true for you, comes a great inner peace. You experience that richness lies within, in the quality of life, and you are attracted to a more simple lifestyle. This is one expression of your new-found liberation and it is accompanied by a deep inner joy. Without feeling the need to communicate this verbally to others, you find that by being just that sort of person you affect others around you and in this way you are bringing about the Kingdom of God in your midst.

Sources

Aron, Elaine and Arthur. *The Maharishi Effect: A Revolution through Meditation.* Stillpoint Publishing, USA, 1986.

Berry, Thomas. *The Dream of the Earth.* The Sierra Club, San Francisco, 1988.

Boff, Leonardo. *Jesus Christ Liberator.* SPCK, London, 1980.
The Church: Charism and Power. SPCK, London, 1984.

Bonhoeffer, Dietrich. *Letters and Papers from Prison.* SCM Press, London, 1981.

Cohen, J.M. & J-F. Phipps. *The Common Experience.* Rider & Co. London, 1979.

Crick, Francis. *The Astonishing Hypothesis: The Scientific Search for the Soul.* Simon & Schuster, London, 1994.

Crossan, John Dominic. *Jesus: A Revolutionary Biography.* Harper, San Francisco, 1994.
Who Killed Jesus? Harper, San Francisco, 1995.

Cuming, Kenneth. *God and the New Age.* A Michael Link Publication, 1975.

Cupitt, Don. *The World to Come.* SCM Press, London, 1982.

Davies, Paul. *The Fifth Miracle.* Allen Lane, London, 1998.

Documents of the Second Vatican Council. Ed. W. Abbott. Geoffrey Chapman, London, 1996:

AA: The Apostolate of the Laity

AG: Missions

DH: Religious Freedom

GS: The Church in the Modern World

LG: The Church

Edwards, Denis. *Creation, Humanity, Community: Building a New Theology.* Gill and Macmillan, Dublin, 1992.

Eisler, Riane. *The Chalice and the Blade.* Harper, San Francisco, 1988.

Elgin, Duane. *Collective Consciousness and Cultural Healing.* Millennium Project, San Anselmo, CA. 1997.

Enomiya-Lassalle, Hugo. *Living in the New Consciousness.* Shambhala, Shaftesbury, 1988.

Griffiths, Bede. *Return to the Centre.* Collins, London, 1976. *Transcending Dualism.* Lecture in Jerusalem, 1983.

A New Vision of Reality. Collins, London, 1989

Hanson, A.T. & R.P.C. *Reasonable Belief.* OUP. 1980.

Harvey, Andrew. *Son of Man.* Tarcher-Putnam, New York, 1998.

Hay, David. *Religious Experience Today.* Mowbray, London, 1990.

Hick, John. *The Fifth Dimension.* One World, Oxford, 1999.

Journal of Consciousness Studies. Imprint Academic. Exeter.

Lamet, Pedro Miguel. *Pedro Arrupe.* Editrice Ancora, Milan, 1993. (quoted in *His Holiness.* Carl Bernstein. Bantam Books, London)

Lovelock, James. *Gaia: A New Look at Life on Earth.* OUP, 1979.

Macquarrie, John. *Principles of Christian Theology.* SCM Press, London, 1977.

Marion, Jim. *Putting on the Mind of Christ.* Hampton Roads, USA, 2000.

MacNulty, Kirk. *UK Social Change through a Wide-angle lens.* World Goodwill, London, 1986.

Naisbitt, John. *Megatrends.* Warner Books. New York, 1982.

New Economics Foundation. *Community Works.* 112 Whitechapel Rd, London E1.

Pannenberg, Wolfhard. *Theology and the Kingdom of God.* Westminster Press, Philadelphia, 1977.

Papal documents:

EN: Evangelisation in the Modern World. Paul VI. 1975.

PP: The Development of Peoples. Paul VI. 1967.

PT: Peace on Earth. John XXIII. 1962.

RM: The Church's Mission. John Paul II. 1990.

Riley, Gregory J. *One Jesus, Many Christs*. Harper, San Francisco, 1997.

Rinpoche, Sogyal. *The Tibetan Book of Living and Dying*. Rider, London, 1992.

Rogers, Paul. *Losing Control: Global Security in the Twenty-first Century*, Pluto Press, 2000.

Russell, Peter. *The Awakening Earth*. Routledge & Kegan Paul, London, 1982.

Schweitzer, Albert. *The Mysticism of Paul the Apostle*. Macmillan, New York, 1955.

Shlain, Leonard. *The Alphabet Versus the Goddess*. Penguine—Arkana, London, 1998.

Smith, Adrian. *The God Shift: Our Changing Perception of the Ultimate Mystery*. New Millennium, London, 1996.
A New Framework for Christian Belief. John Hunt Publishing, UK. 2002.

Spong, John Shelby. *Resurrection: Myth or Reality?* Harper, San Francisco, 1994.

Teilhard de Chardin, Pierre. *The Future of Man*. Collins, London, 1964.
Science and Christ. Collins, London, 1968.
Christianity and Evolution. Collins, London, 1969.

Trevelyan, Sir George. *A Vision of the Aquarian Age*. Coventure, London, 1977.

Wink, Walter. *The Powers That Be*. Doubleday, London, 1998.

Wilber, Ken. *A Brief History of Everything*. Gill & Macmillan, Dublin, 1996.

World Council of Churches. *The Church for Others*. WCC, Geneva, 1968.